ARSENAL
THE COMIC STRIP HISTORY

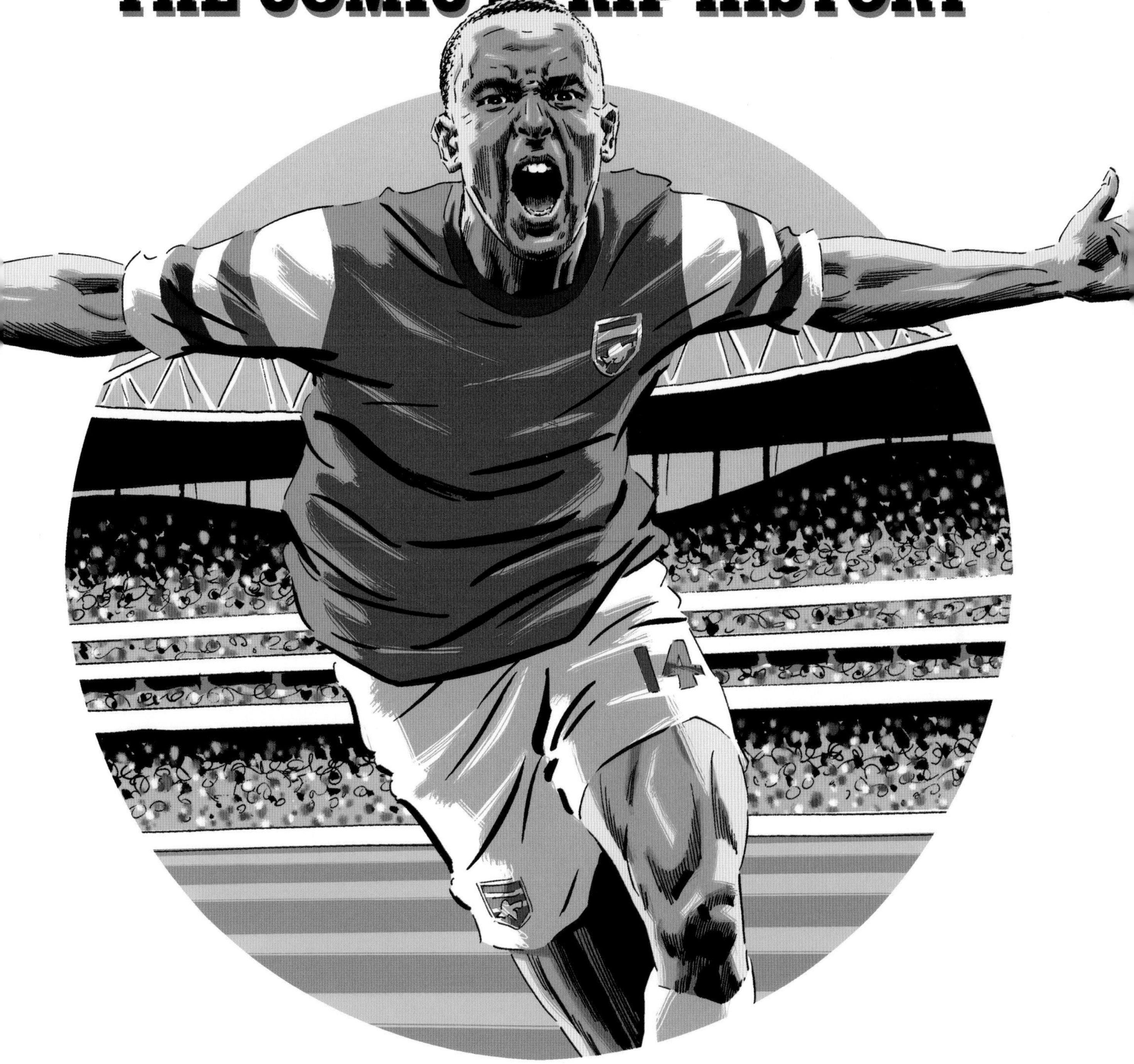
14

Published by Vision Sports Publishing Limited in 2013

Vision Sports Publishing Ltd
19-23 High Street
Kingston upon Thames
Surrey
KT1 1LL
www.visionsp.co.uk

© Bob Bond

ISBN: 978-1909534-13-1

This book is 100 per cent unofficial

Art and script: Bob Bond
Cover artwork: Stephen Gulbis
Cover design: Neal Cobourne
Editor: Jim Drewett
Production Editor: John Murray

Printed in China by Hung Hing

A CIP Catalogue record for this book is available from the British Library

BOB BOND

Caricatures of many of the legendary Arsenal players drawn by this book's illustrator, Bob Bond, can be purchased, as postcards or A3 and A4 prints. Email **bobbond@live.co.uk** for a list of players available. Excellent as gift ideas, for autographing, or to add to your personal memorabilia collection.

STEPHEN GULBIS

Football and art prints by Stephen Gulbis are available from **www.thefootballartist.com**

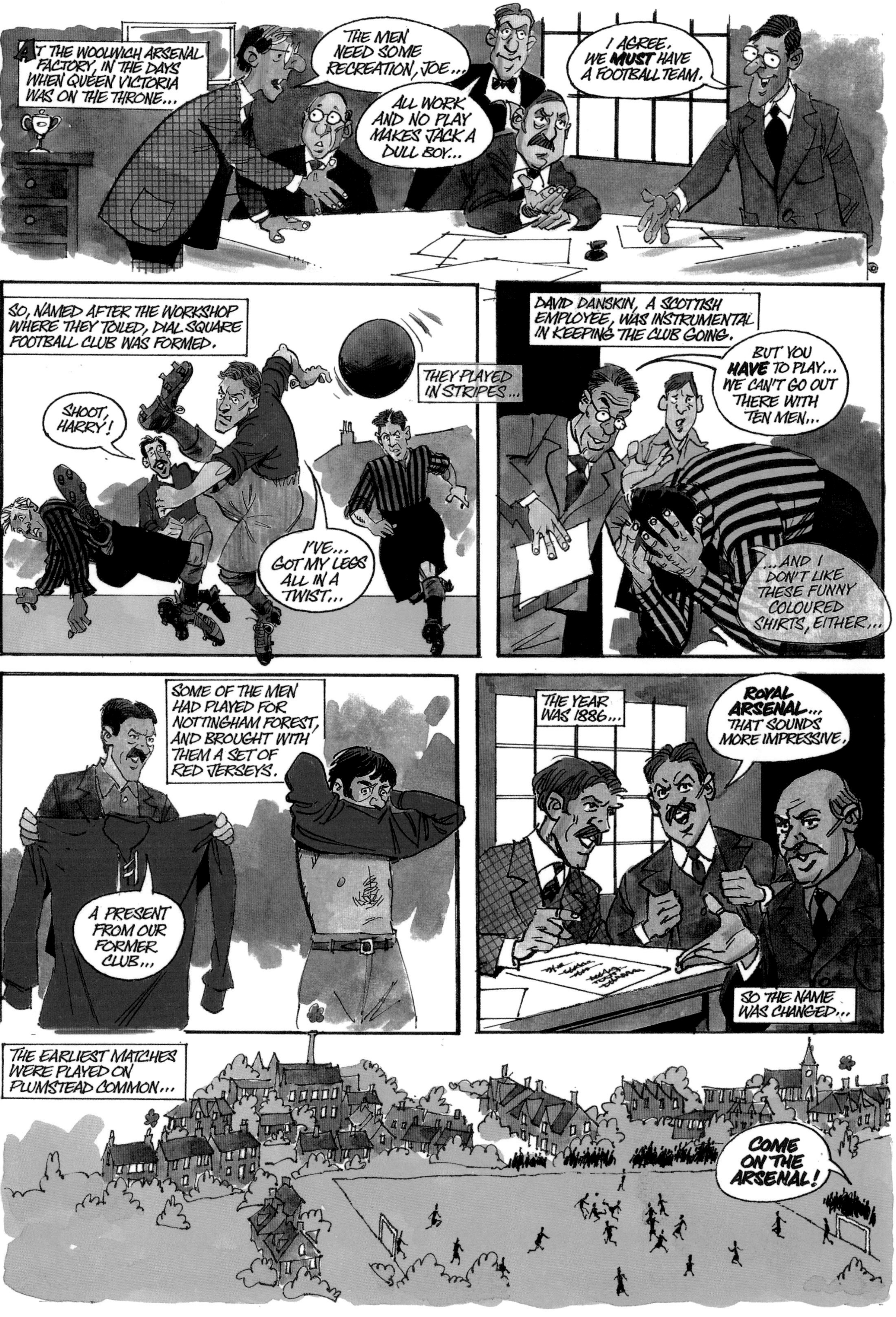
AT THE WOOLWICH ARSENAL FACTORY, IN THE DAYS WHEN QUEEN VICTORIA WAS ON THE THRONE...
THE MEN NEED SOME RECREATION, JOE...
ALL WORK AND NO PLAY MAKES JACK A DULL BOY...
I AGREE. WE MUST HAVE A FOOTBALL TEAM.
SO, NAMED AFTER THE WORKSHOP WHERE THEY TOILED, DIAL SQUARE FOOTBALL CLUB WAS FORMED.
SHOOT, HARRY!
THEY PLAYED IN STRIPES...
I'VE... GOT MY LEGS ALL IN A TWIST...
DAVID DANSKIN, A SCOTTISH EMPLOYEE, WAS INSTRUMENTAL IN KEEPING THE CLUB GOING.
BUT YOU HAVE TO PLAY... WE CAN'T GO OUT THERE WITH TEN MEN...
...AND I DON'T LIKE THESE FUNNY COLOURED SHIRTS, EITHER...
SOME OF THE MEN HAD PLAYED FOR NOTTINGHAM FOREST, AND BROUGHT WITH THEM A SET OF RED JERSEYS.
A PRESENT FROM OUR FORMER CLUB...
THE YEAR WAS 1886...
ROYAL ARSENAL... THAT SOUNDS MORE IMPRESSIVE.
SO THE NAME WAS CHANGED...
THE EARLIEST MATCHES WERE PLAYED ON PLUMSTEAD COMMON...
COME ON THE ARSENAL!

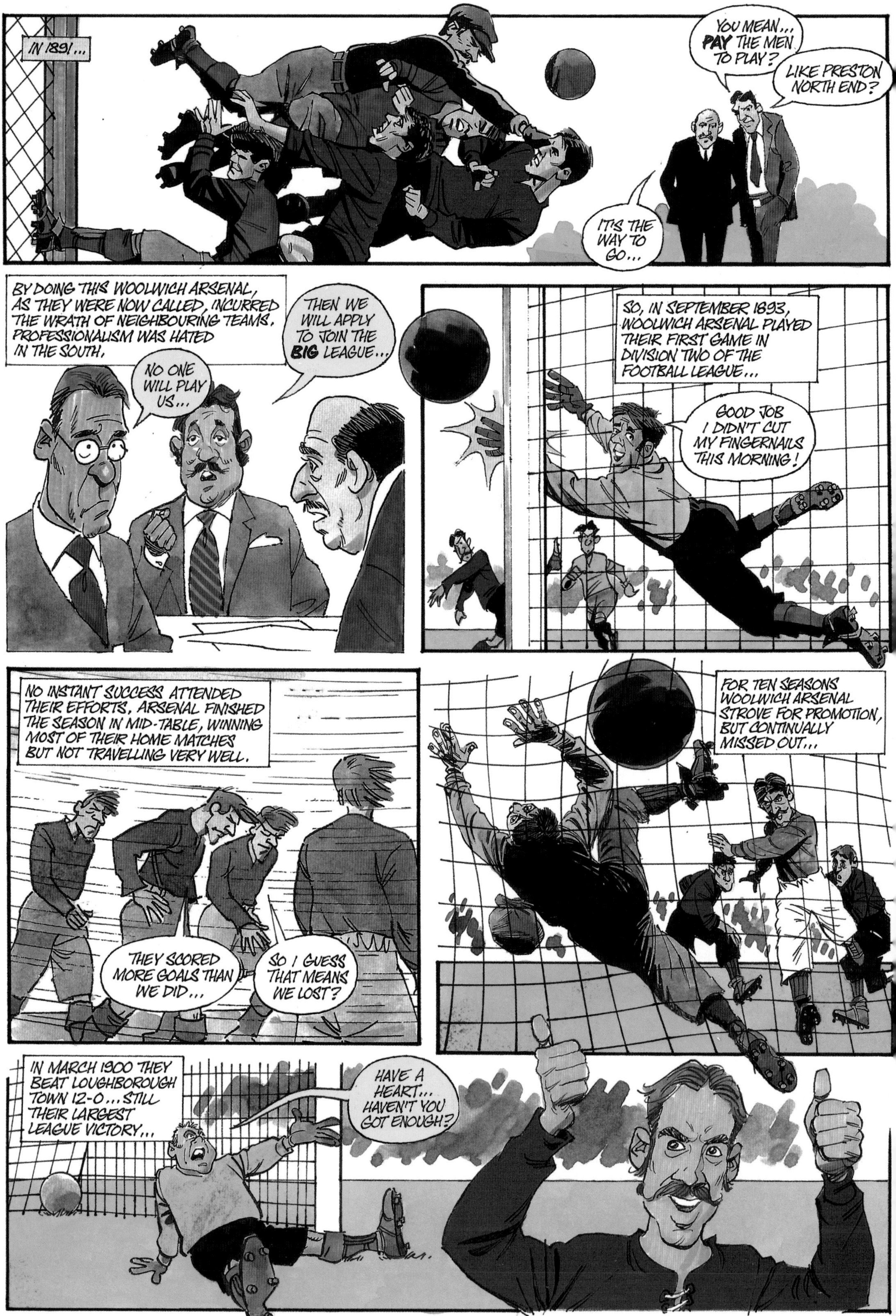
IN 1891...
YOU MEAN... PAY THE MEN TO PLAY?
LIKE PRESTON NORTH END?
IT'S THE WAY TO GO...
BY DOING THIS WOOLWICH ARSENAL, AS THEY WERE NOW CALLED, INCURRED THE WRATH OF NEIGHBOURING TEAMS. PROFESSIONALISM WAS HATED IN THE SOUTH.
NO ONE WILL PLAY US...
THEN WE WILL APPLY TO JOIN THE BIG LEAGUE...
SO, IN SEPTEMBER 1893, WOOLWICH ARSENAL PLAYED THEIR FIRST GAME IN DIVISION TWO OF THE FOOTBALL LEAGUE...
GOOD JOB I DIDN'T CUT MY FINGERNAILS THIS MORNING!
NO INSTANT SUCCESS ATTENDED THEIR EFFORTS. ARSENAL FINISHED THE SEASON IN MID-TABLE, WINNING MOST OF THEIR HOME MATCHES BUT NOT TRAVELLING VERY WELL.
THEY SCORED MORE GOALS THAN WE DID...
SO I GUESS THAT MEANS WE LOST?
FOR TEN SEASONS WOOLWICH ARSENAL STROVE FOR PROMOTION, BUT CONTINUALLY MISSED OUT...
IN MARCH 1900 THEY BEAT LOUGHBOROUGH TOWN 12-0... STILL THEIR LARGEST LEAGUE VICTORY...
HAVE A HEART... HAVEN'T YOU GOT ENOUGH?

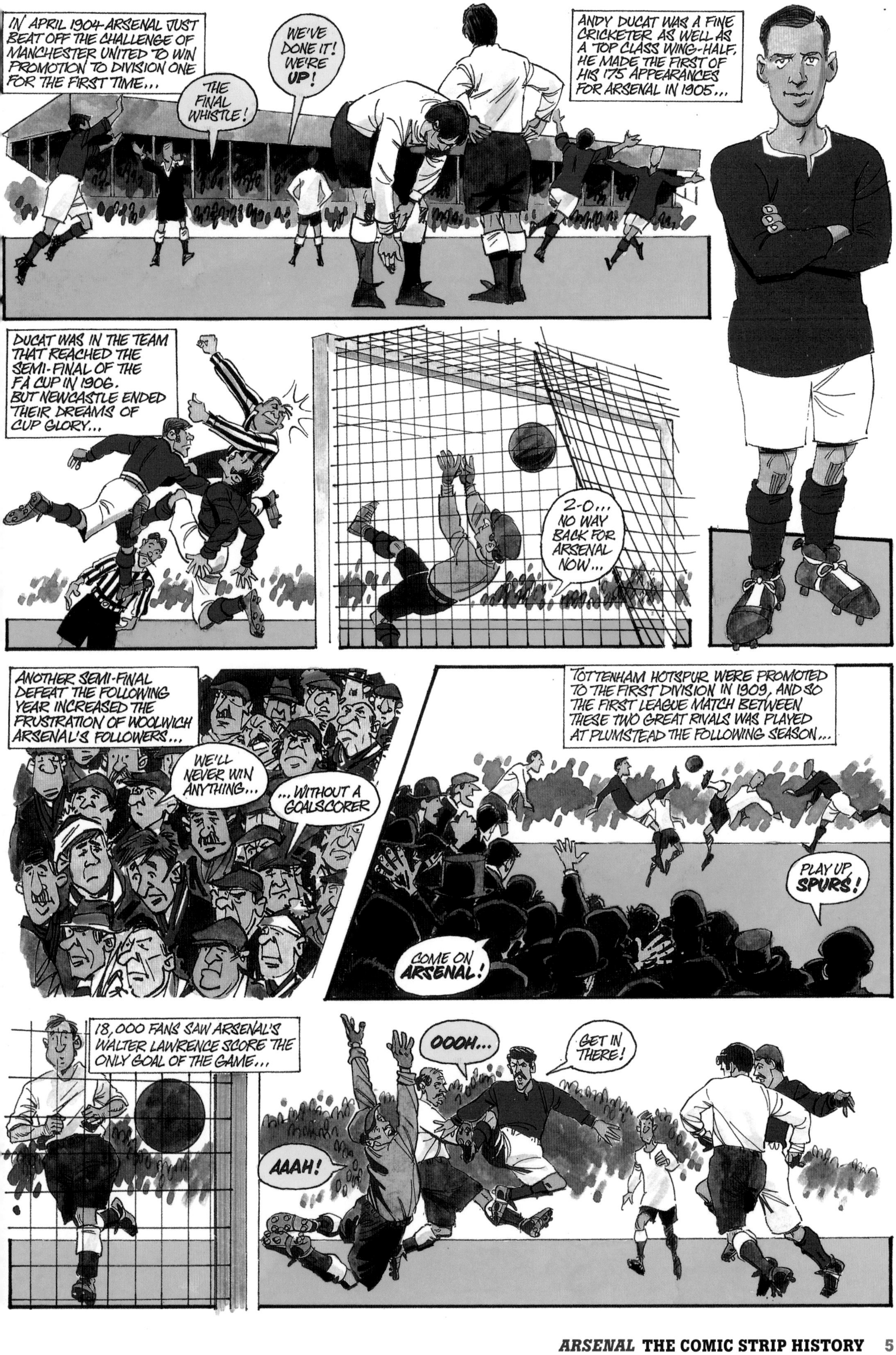

IN APRIL 1904 ARSENAL JUST BEAT OFF THE CHALLENGE OF MANCHESTER UNITED TO WIN PROMOTION TO DIVISION ONE FOR THE FIRST TIME...
THE FINAL WHISTLE!
WE'VE DONE IT! WE'RE UP!
ANDY DUCAT WAS A FINE CRICKETER AS WELL AS A TOP CLASS WING-HALF. HE MADE THE FIRST OF HIS 175 APPEARANCES FOR ARSENAL IN 1905...
DUCAT WAS IN THE TEAM THAT REACHED THE SEMI-FINAL OF THE FA CUP IN 1906. BUT NEWCASTLE ENDED THEIR DREAMS OF CUP GLORY...
2-0... NO WAY BACK FOR ARSENAL NOW...
ANOTHER SEMI-FINAL DEFEAT THE FOLLOWING YEAR INCREASED THE FRUSTRATION OF WOOLWICH ARSENAL'S FOLLOWERS...
WE'LL NEVER WIN ANYTHING...
...WITHOUT A GOALSCORER
TOTTENHAM HOTSPUR WERE PROMOTED TO THE FIRST DIVISION IN 1909, AND SO THE FIRST LEAGUE MATCH BETWEEN THESE TWO GREAT RIVALS WAS PLAYED AT PLUMSTEAD THE FOLLOWING SEASON...
PLAY UP, SPURS!
COME ON ARSENAL!
18,000 FANS SAW ARSENAL'S WALTER LAWRENCE SCORE THE ONLY GOAL OF THE GAME...
OOOH...
GET IN THERE!
AAAH!

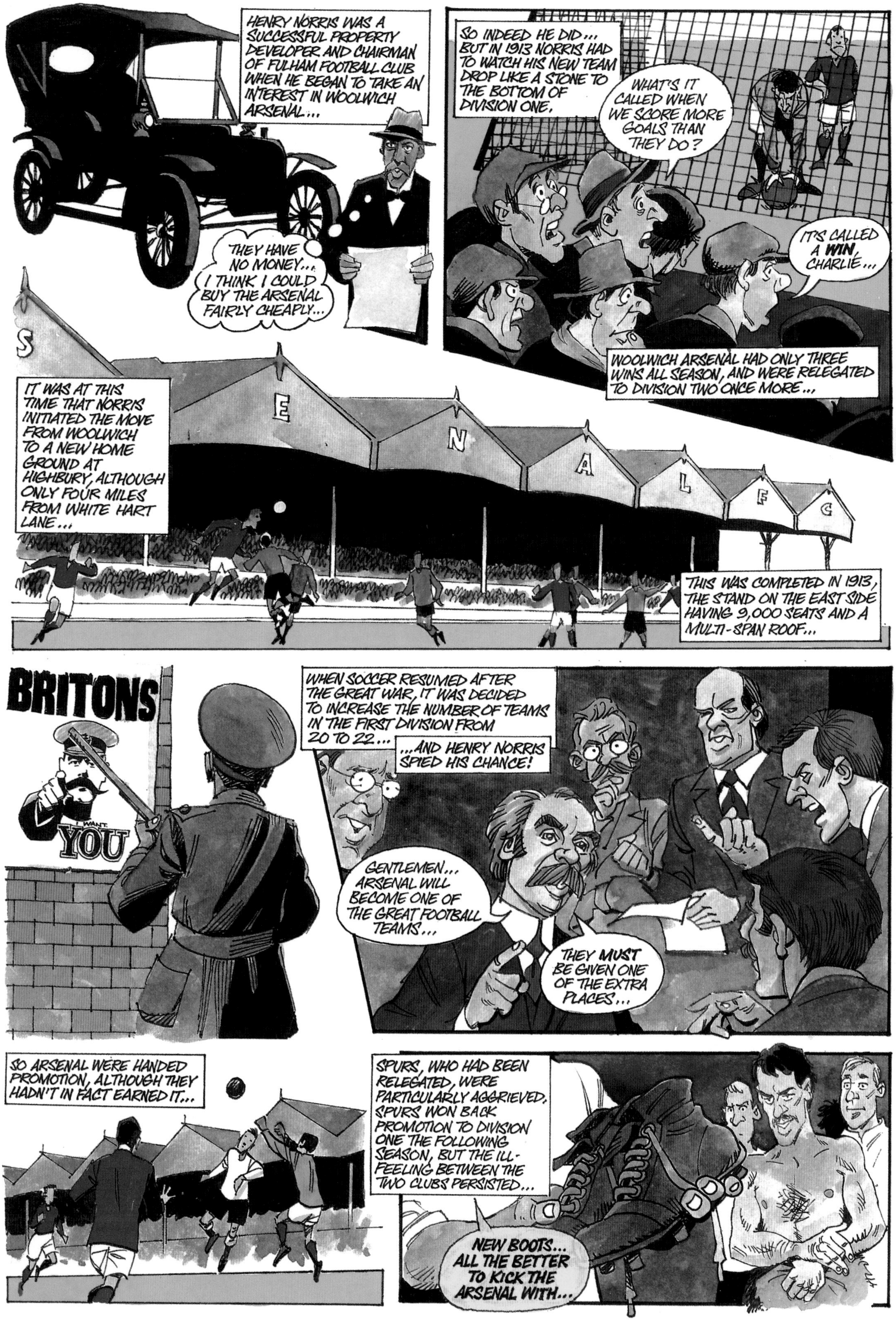
HENRY NORRIS WAS A SUCCESSFUL PROPERTY DEVELOPER AND CHAIRMAN OF FULHAM FOOTBALL CLUB WHEN HE BEGAN TO TAKE AN INTEREST IN WOOLWICH ARSENAL...
THEY HAVE NO MONEY... I THINK I COULD BUY THE ARSENAL FAIRLY CHEAPLY...
SO INDEED HE DID... BUT IN 1913 NORRIS HAD TO WATCH HIS NEW TEAM DROP LIKE A STONE TO THE BOTTOM OF DIVISION ONE.
WHAT'S IT CALLED WHEN WE SCORE MORE GOALS THAN THEY DO?
IT'S CALLED A **WIN**, CHARLIE...
WOOLWICH ARSENAL HAD ONLY THREE WINS ALL SEASON, AND WERE RELEGATED TO DIVISION TWO ONCE MORE...
IT WAS AT THIS TIME THAT NORRIS INITIATED THE MOVE FROM WOOLWICH TO A NEW HOME GROUND AT HIGHBURY, ALTHOUGH ONLY FOUR MILES FROM WHITE HART LANE...
S E N A L F C
THIS WAS COMPLETED IN 1913, THE STAND ON THE EAST SIDE HAVING 9,000 SEATS AND A MULTI-SPAN ROOF...
BRITONS
I WANT YOU
WHEN SOCCER RESUMED AFTER THE GREAT WAR, IT WAS DECIDED TO INCREASE THE NUMBER OF TEAMS IN THE FIRST DIVISION FROM 20 TO 22...
...AND HENRY NORRIS SPIED HIS CHANCE!
GENTLEMEN... ARSENAL WILL BECOME ONE OF THE GREAT FOOTBALL TEAMS...
THEY **MUST** BE GIVEN ONE OF THE EXTRA PLACES...
SO ARSENAL WERE HANDED PROMOTION, ALTHOUGH THEY HADN'T IN FACT EARNED IT...
SPURS, WHO HAD BEEN RELEGATED, WERE PARTICULARLY AGGRIEVED. SPURS WON BACK PROMOTION TO DIVISION ONE THE FOLLOWING SEASON, BUT THE ILL-FEELING BETWEEN THE TWO CLUBS PERSISTED...
NEW BOOTS... ALL THE BETTER TO KICK THE ARSENAL WITH...

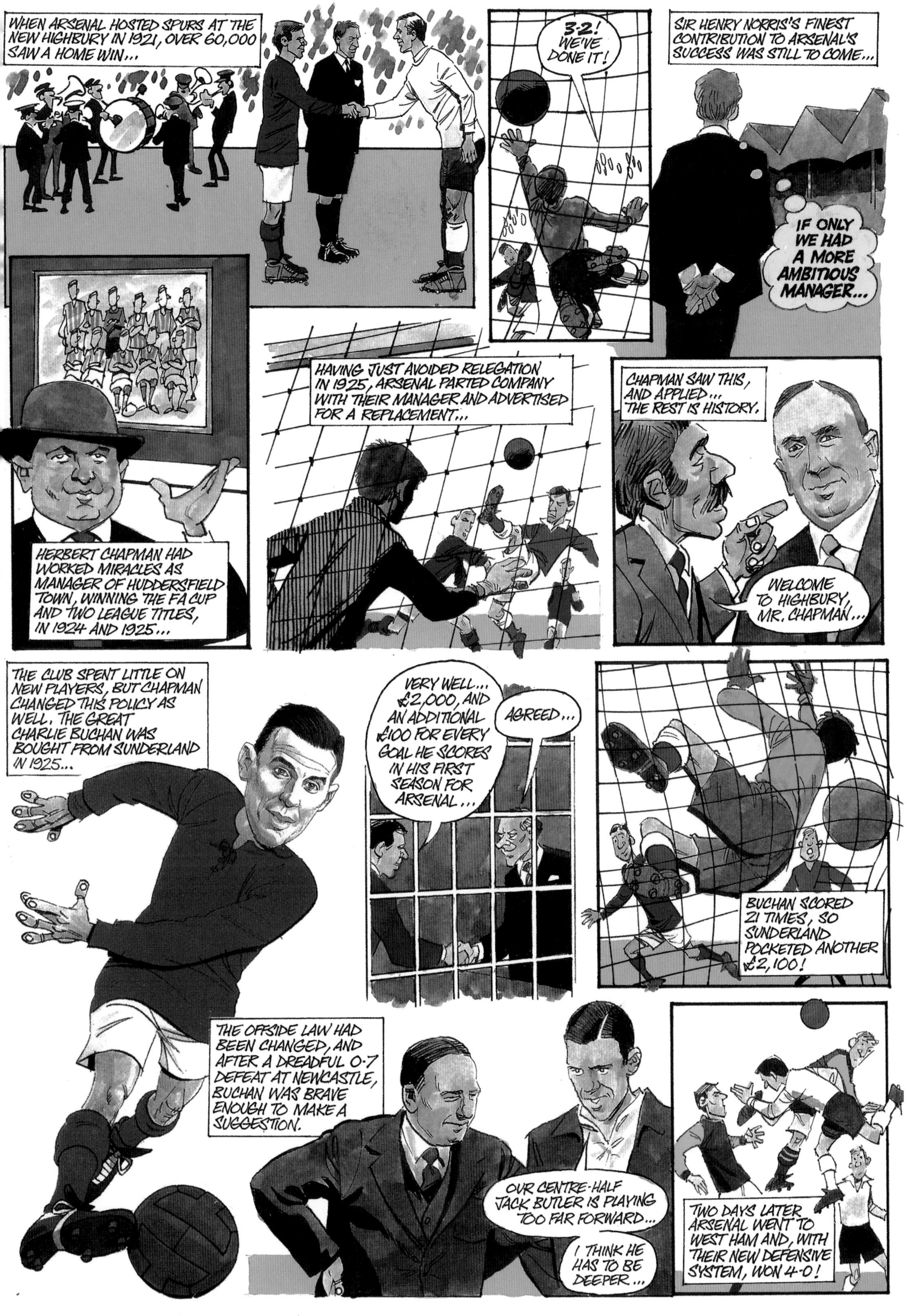
WHEN ARSENAL HOSTED SPURS AT THE NEW HIGHBURY IN 1921, OVER 60,000 SAW A HOME WIN...
3-2! WE'VE DONE IT!
SIR HENRY NORRIS'S FINEST CONTRIBUTION TO ARSENAL'S SUCCESS WAS STILL TO COME...
IF ONLY WE HAD A MORE AMBITIOUS MANAGER...
HERBERT CHAPMAN HAD WORKED MIRACLES AS MANAGER OF HUDDERSFIELD TOWN, WINNING THE FA CUP AND TWO LEAGUE TITLES, IN 1924 AND 1925...
HAVING JUST AVOIDED RELEGATION IN 1925, ARSENAL PARTED COMPANY WITH THEIR MANAGER AND ADVERTISED FOR A REPLACEMENT...
CHAPMAN SAW THIS, AND APPLIED... THE REST IS HISTORY.
WELCOME TO HIGHBURY, MR. CHAPMAN...
THE CLUB SPENT LITTLE ON NEW PLAYERS, BUT CHAPMAN CHANGED THIS POLICY AS WELL. THE GREAT CHARLIE BUCHAN WAS BOUGHT FROM SUNDERLAND IN 1925...
VERY WELL... £2,000, AND AN ADDITIONAL £100 FOR EVERY GOAL HE SCORES IN HIS FIRST SEASON FOR ARSENAL...
AGREED...
BUCHAN SCORED 21 TIMES, SO SUNDERLAND POCKETED ANOTHER £2,100!
THE OFFSIDE LAW HAD BEEN CHANGED, AND AFTER A DREADFUL 0-7 DEFEAT AT NEWCASTLE, BUCHAN WAS BRAVE ENOUGH TO MAKE A SUGGESTION.
OUR CENTRE-HALF JACK BUTLER IS PLAYING TOO FAR FORWARD...
I THINK HE HAS TO BE DEEPER...
TWO DAYS LATER ARSENAL WENT TO WEST HAM AND, WITH THEIR NEW DEFENSIVE SYSTEM, WON 4-0!

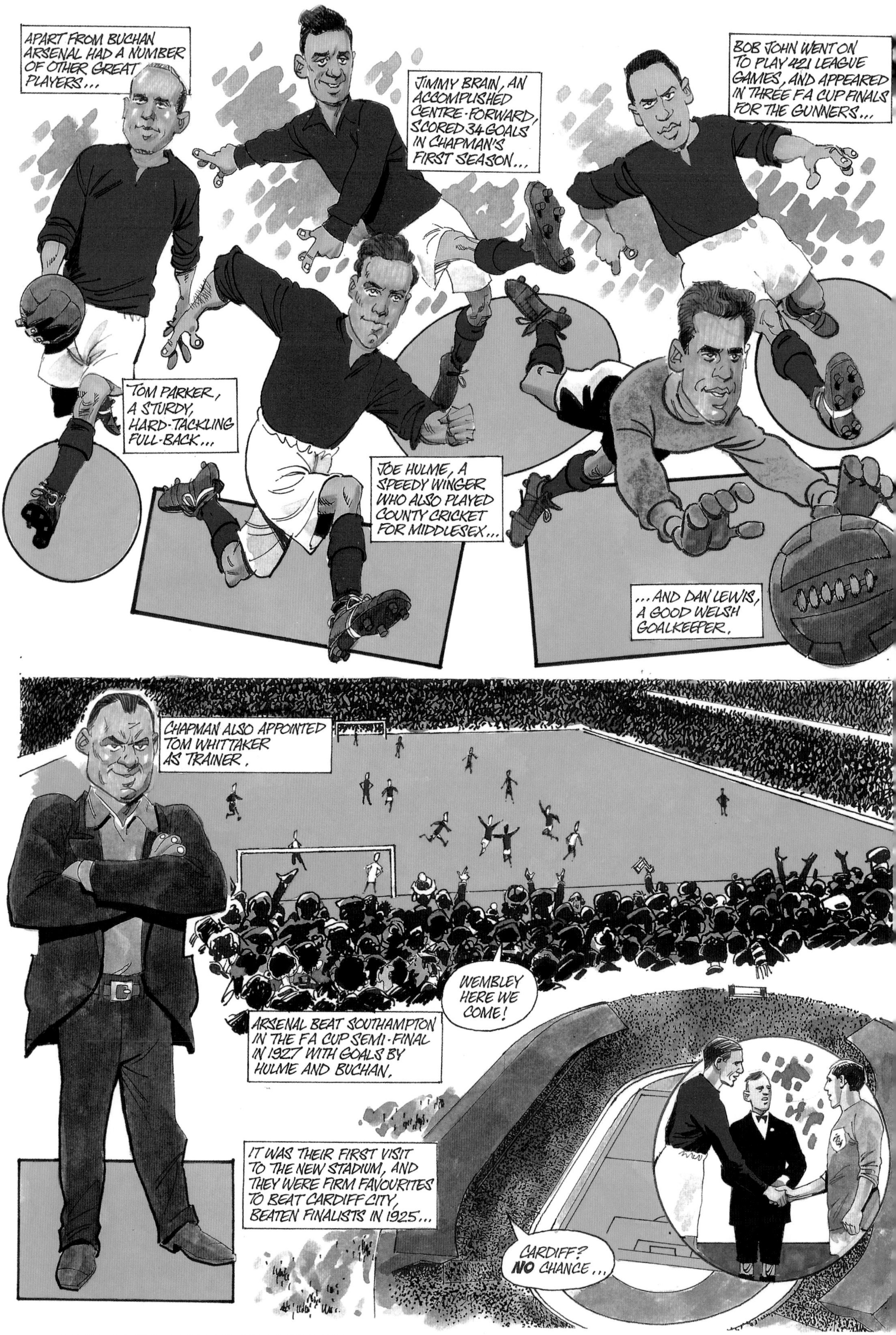
APART FROM BUCHAN ARSENAL HAD A NUMBER OF OTHER GREAT PLAYERS...
JIMMY BRAIN, AN ACCOMPLISHED CENTRE-FORWARD, SCORED 34 GOALS IN CHAPMAN'S FIRST SEASON...
BOB JOHN WENT ON TO PLAY 421 LEAGUE GAMES, AND APPEARED IN THREE FA CUP FINALS FOR THE GUNNERS...
TOM PARKER, A STURDY, HARD-TACKLING FULL-BACK...
JOE HULME, A SPEEDY WINGER WHO ALSO PLAYED COUNTY CRICKET FOR MIDDLESEX...
...AND DAN LEWIS, A GOOD WELSH GOALKEEPER.
CHAPMAN ALSO APPOINTED TOM WHITTAKER AS TRAINER.
WEMBLEY HERE WE COME!
ARSENAL BEAT SOUTHAMPTON IN THE FA CUP SEMI-FINAL IN 1927 WITH GOALS BY HULME AND BUCHAN.
IT WAS THEIR FIRST VISIT TO THE NEW STADIUM, AND THEY WERE FIRM FAVOURITES TO BEAT CARDIFF CITY, BEATEN FINALISTS IN 1925...
CARDIFF? NO CHANCE...

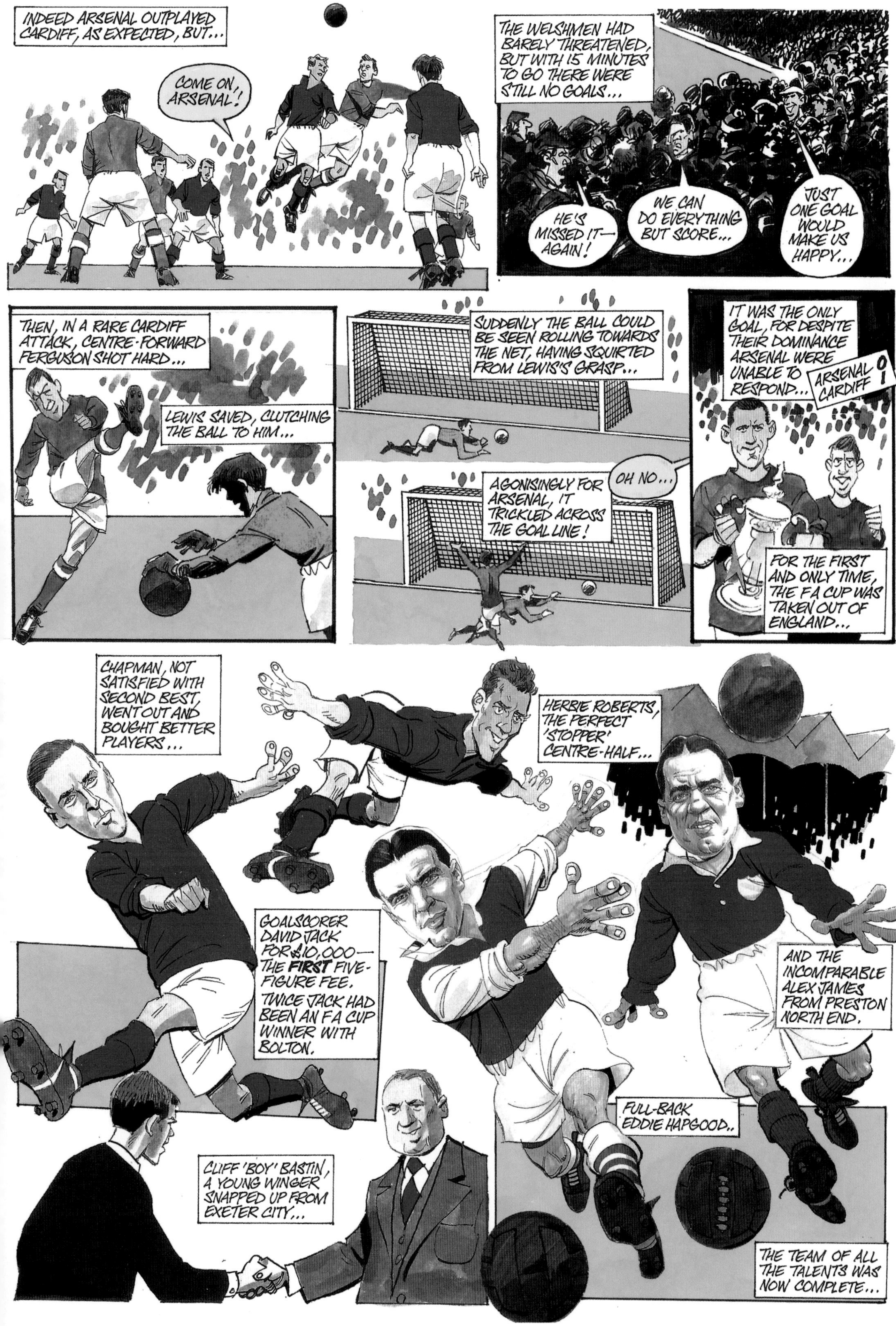
INDEED ARSENAL OUTPLAYED CARDIFF, AS EXPECTED, BUT...
COME ON, ARSENAL!
THE WELSHMEN HAD BARELY THREATENED, BUT WITH 15 MINUTES TO GO THERE WERE STILL NO GOALS...
HE'S MISSED IT— AGAIN!
WE CAN DO EVERYTHING BUT SCORE...
JUST ONE GOAL WOULD MAKE US HAPPY...
THEN, IN A RARE CARDIFF ATTACK, CENTRE-FORWARD FERGUSON SHOT HARD...
LEWIS SAVED, CLUTCHING THE BALL TO HIM...
SUDDENLY THE BALL COULD BE SEEN ROLLING TOWARDS THE NET, HAVING SQUIRTED FROM LEWIS'S GRASP...
AGONISINGLY FOR ARSENAL, IT TRICKLED ACROSS THE GOAL LINE!
OH NO...
IT WAS THE ONLY GOAL, FOR DESPITE THEIR DOMINANCE ARSENAL WERE UNABLE TO RESPOND...
ARSENAL 0
CARDIFF 1
FOR THE FIRST AND ONLY TIME, THE FA CUP WAS TAKEN OUT OF ENGLAND...
CHAPMAN, NOT SATISFIED WITH SECOND BEST, WENT OUT AND BOUGHT BETTER PLAYERS...
HERBIE ROBERTS, THE PERFECT 'STOPPER' CENTRE-HALF...
GOALSCORER DAVID JACK FOR £10,000— THE FIRST FIVE-FIGURE FEE.
TWICE JACK HAD BEEN AN FA CUP WINNER WITH BOLTON.
AND THE INCOMPARABLE ALEX JAMES FROM PRESTON NORTH END.
FULL-BACK EDDIE HAPGOOD..
CLIFF 'BOY' BASTIN, A YOUNG WINGER SNAPPED UP FROM EXETER CITY...
THE TEAM OF ALL THE TALENTS WAS NOW COMPLETE...

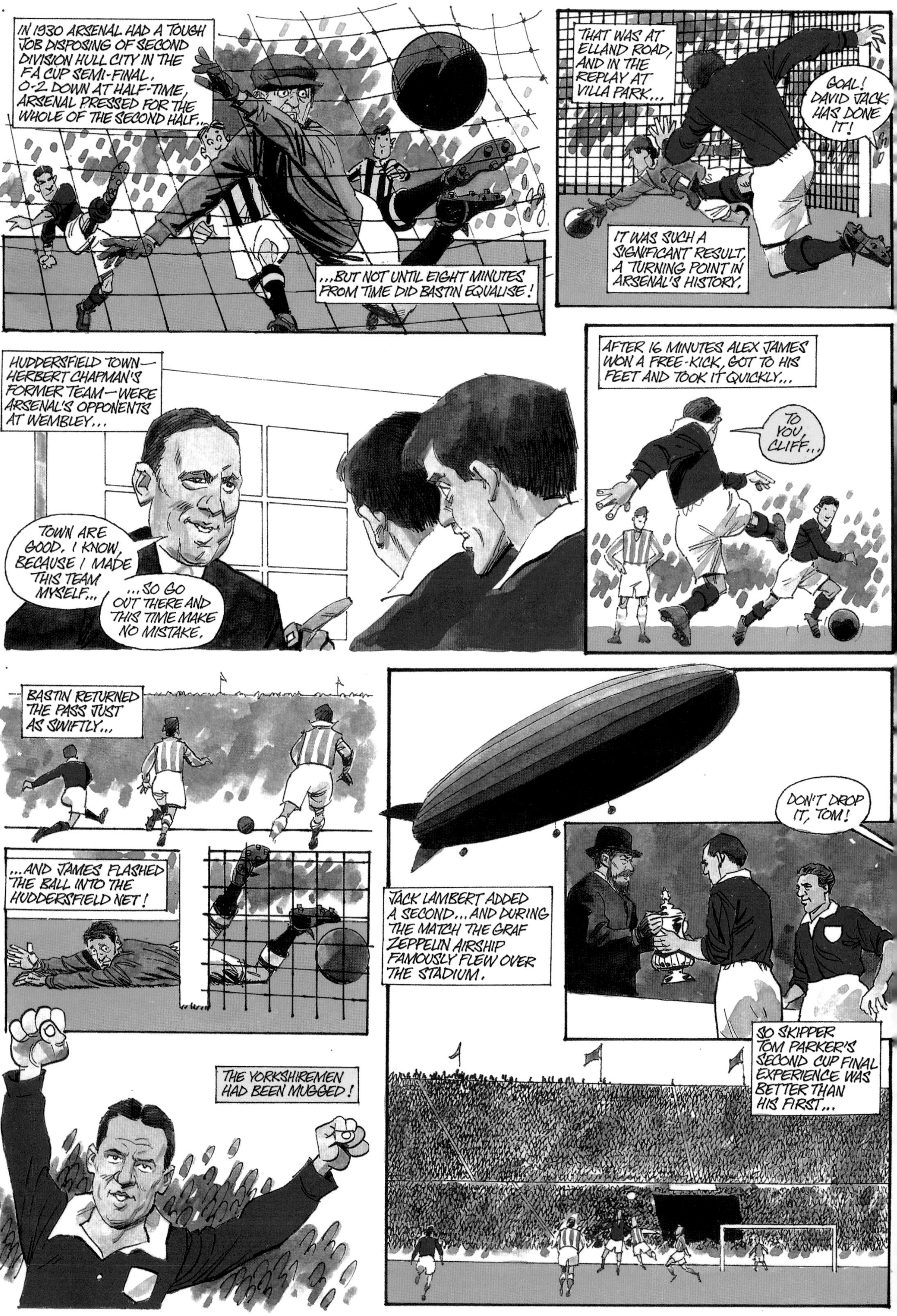
IN 1930 ARSENAL HAD A TOUGH JOB DISPOSING OF SECOND DIVISION HULL CITY IN THE FA CUP SEMI-FINAL. 0-2 DOWN AT HALF-TIME, ARSENAL PRESSED FOR THE WHOLE OF THE SECOND HALF...
...BUT NOT UNTIL EIGHT MINUTES FROM TIME DID BASTIN EQUALISE!
THAT WAS AT ELLAND ROAD, AND IN THE REPLAY AT VILLA PARK...
GOAL! DAVID JACK HAS DONE IT!
IT WAS SUCH A SIGNIFICANT RESULT, A TURNING POINT IN ARSENAL'S HISTORY.
HUDDERSFIELD TOWN—HERBERT CHAPMAN'S FORMER TEAM—WERE ARSENAL'S OPPONENTS AT WEMBLEY...
TOWN ARE GOOD. I KNOW, BECAUSE I MADE THIS TEAM MYSELF...
...SO GO OUT THERE AND THIS TIME MAKE NO MISTAKE.
AFTER 16 MINUTES ALEX JAMES WON A FREE-KICK, GOT TO HIS FEET AND TOOK IT QUICKLY...
TO YOU, CLIFF...
BASTIN RETURNED THE PASS JUST AS SWIFTLY...
...AND JAMES FLASHED THE BALL INTO THE HUDDERSFIELD NET!
THE YORKSHIREMEN HAD BEEN MUGGED!
JACK LAMBERT ADDED A SECOND... AND DURING THE MATCH THE GRAF ZEPPELIN AIRSHIP FAMOUSLY FLEW OVER THE STADIUM.
DON'T DROP IT, TOM!
SO SKIPPER TOM PARKER'S SECOND CUP FINAL EXPERIENCE WAS BETTER THAN HIS FIRST...

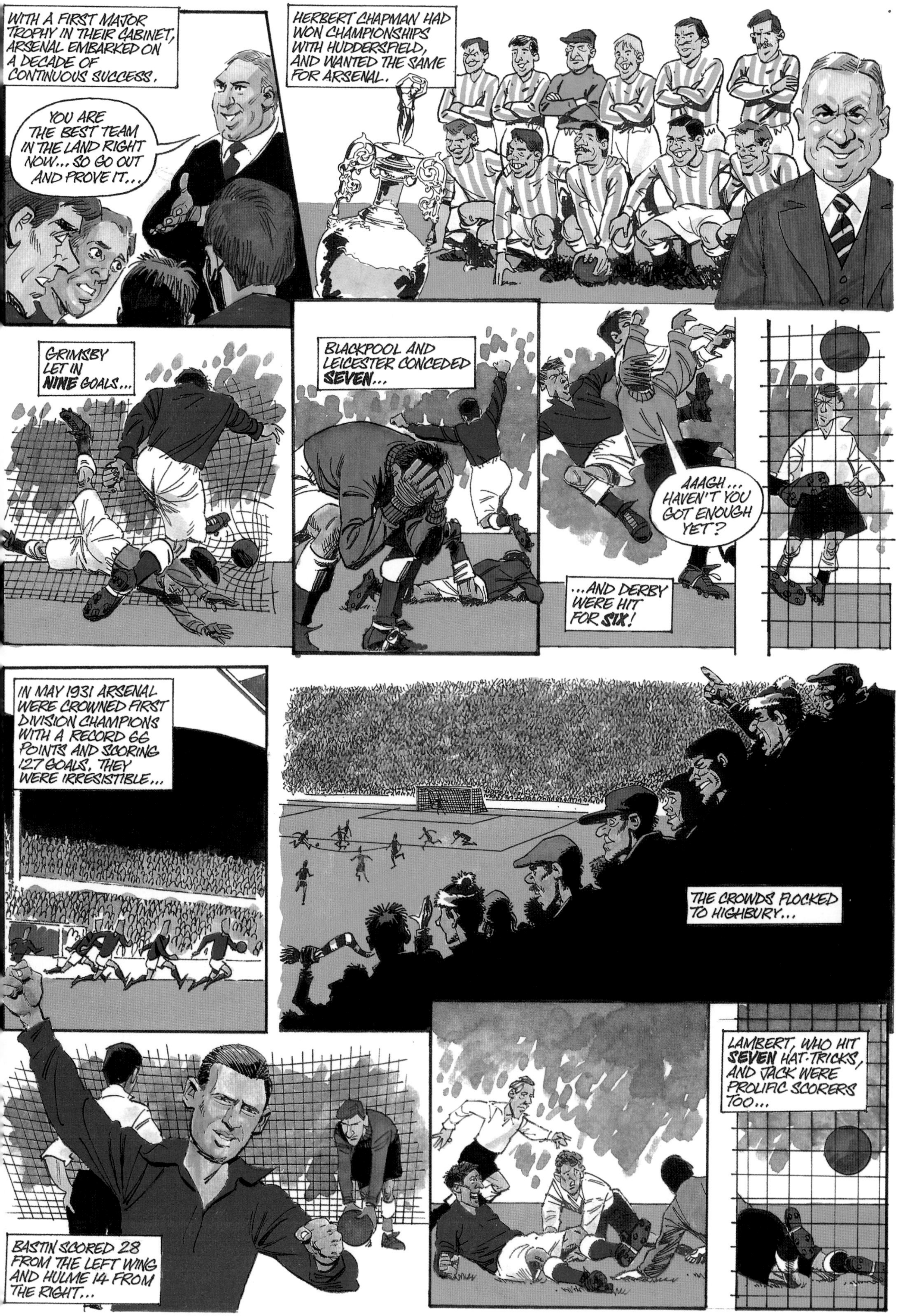
WITH A FIRST MAJOR TROPHY IN THEIR CABINET, ARSENAL EMBARKED ON A DECADE OF CONTINUOUS SUCCESS.
YOU ARE THE BEST TEAM IN THE LAND RIGHT NOW... SO GO OUT AND PROVE IT...
HERBERT CHAPMAN HAD WON CHAMPIONSHIPS WITH HUDDERSFIELD, AND WANTED THE SAME FOR ARSENAL.
GRIMSBY LET IN NINE GOALS...
BLACKPOOL AND LEICESTER CONCEDED SEVEN...
AAAGH... HAVEN'T YOU GOT ENOUGH YET?
...AND DERBY WERE HIT FOR SIX!
IN MAY 1931 ARSENAL WERE CROWNED FIRST DIVISION CHAMPIONS WITH A RECORD 66 POINTS AND SCORING 127 GOALS. THEY WERE IRRESISTIBLE...
THE CROWDS FLOCKED TO HIGHBURY...
BASTIN SCORED 28 FROM THE LEFT WING AND HULME 14 FROM THE RIGHT...
LAMBERT, WHO HIT SEVEN HAT-TRICKS, AND JACK WERE PROLIFIC SCORERS TOO...

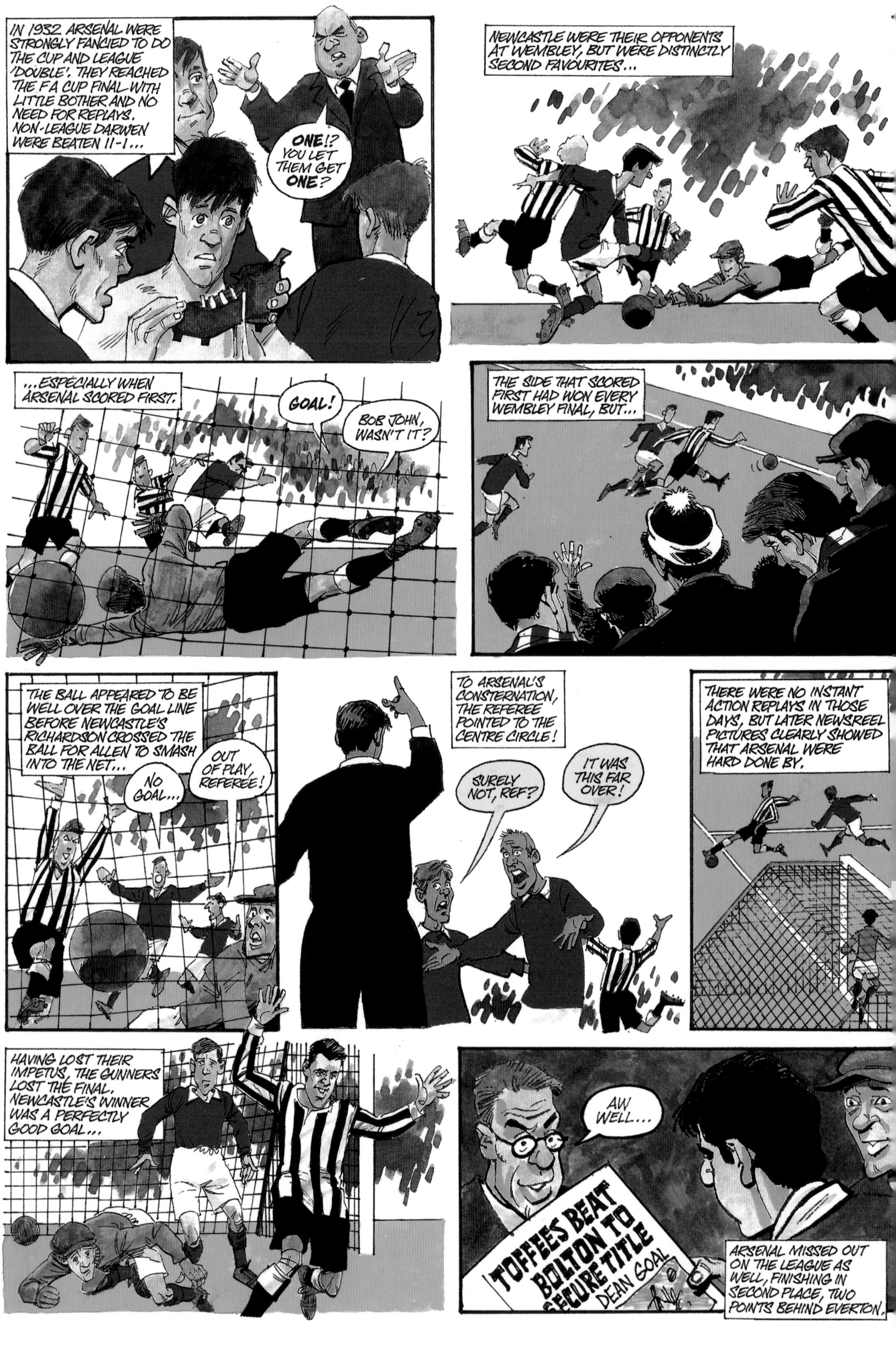
IN 1932 ARSENAL WERE STRONGLY FANCIED TO DO THE CUP AND LEAGUE 'DOUBLE'. THEY REACHED THE F A CUP FINAL WITH LITTLE BOTHER AND NO NEED FOR REPLAYS. NON-LEAGUE DARWEN WERE BEATEN 11-1...
ONE!? YOU LET THEM GET ONE?
NEWCASTLE WERE THEIR OPPONENTS AT WEMBLEY, BUT WERE DISTINCTLY SECOND FAVOURITES...
...ESPECIALLY WHEN ARSENAL SCORED FIRST.
GOAL!
BOB JOHN, WASN'T IT?
THE SIDE THAT SCORED FIRST HAD WON EVERY WEMBLEY FINAL, BUT...
THE BALL APPEARED TO BE WELL OVER THE GOAL LINE BEFORE NEWCASTLE'S RICHARDSON CROSSED THE BALL FOR ALLEN TO SMASH INTO THE NET...
NO GOAL...
OUT OF PLAY, REFEREE!
TO ARSENAL'S CONSTERNATION, THE REFEREE POINTED TO THE CENTRE CIRCLE!
SURELY NOT, REF?
IT WAS THIS FAR OVER!
THERE WERE NO INSTANT ACTION REPLAYS IN THOSE DAYS, BUT LATER NEWSREEL PICTURES CLEARLY SHOWED THAT ARSENAL WERE HARD DONE BY.
HAVING LOST THEIR IMPETUS, THE GUNNERS LOST THE FINAL. NEWCASTLE'S WINNER WAS A PERFECTLY GOOD GOAL...
AW WELL...
TOFFEES BEAT BOLTON TO SECURE TITLE
DEAN GOAL
ARSENAL MISSED OUT ON THE LEAGUE AS WELL, FINISHING IN SECOND PLACE, TWO POINTS BEHIND EVERTON.

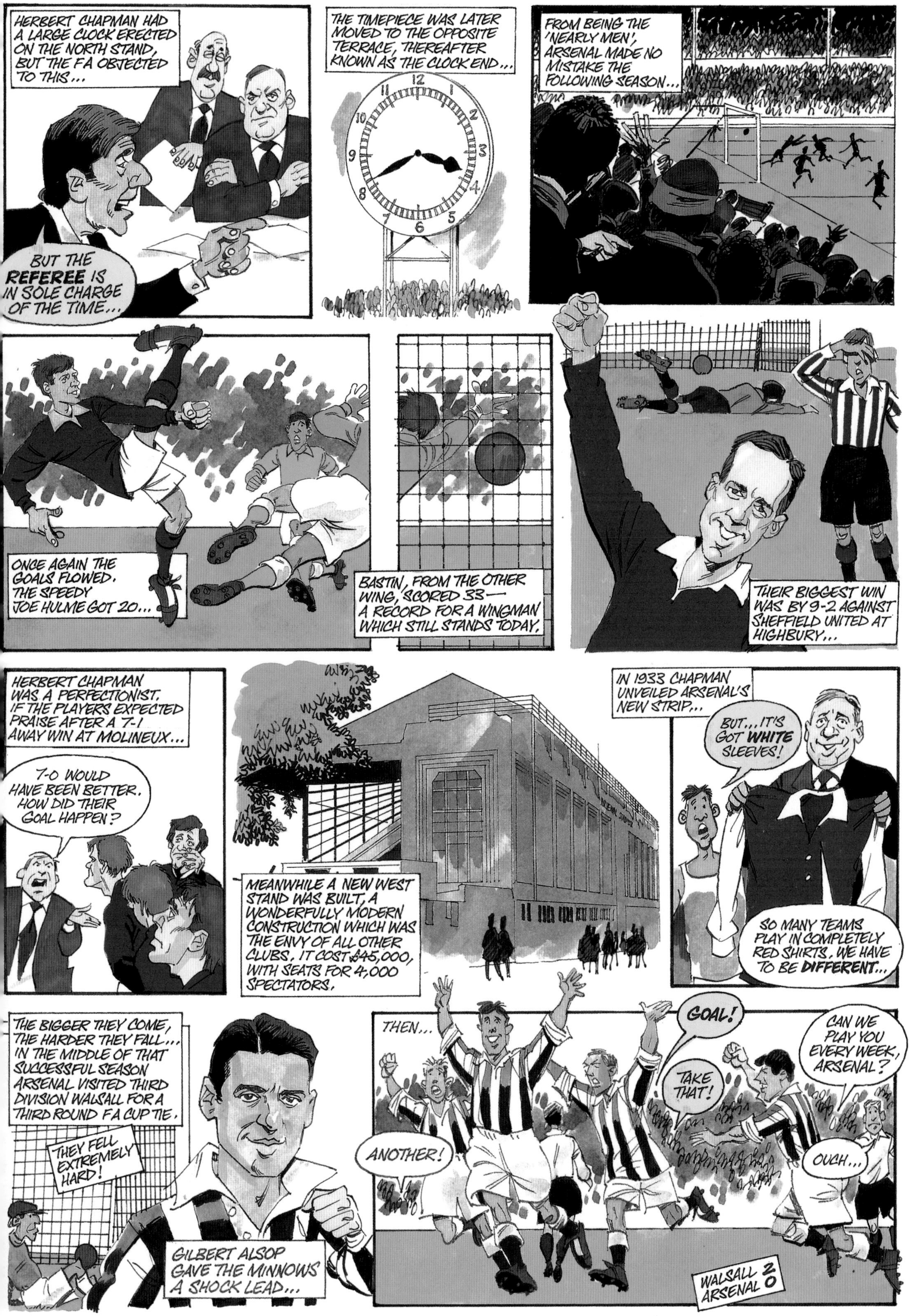
HERBERT CHAPMAN HAD A LARGE CLOCK ERECTED ON THE NORTH STAND, BUT THE FA OBJECTED TO THIS...
BUT THE **REFEREE** IS IN SOLE CHARGE OF THE TIME...
THE TIMEPIECE WAS LATER MOVED TO THE OPPOSITE TERRACE, THEREAFTER KNOWN AS THE CLOCK END...
FROM BEING THE 'NEARLY MEN', ARSENAL MADE NO MISTAKE THE FOLLOWING SEASON...
ONCE AGAIN THE GOALS FLOWED. THE SPEEDY JOE HULME GOT 20...
BASTIN, FROM THE OTHER WING, SCORED 33— A RECORD FOR A WINGMAN WHICH STILL STANDS TODAY.
THEIR BIGGEST WIN WAS BY 9-2 AGAINST SHEFFIELD UNITED AT HIGHBURY...
HERBERT CHAPMAN WAS A PERFECTIONIST. IF THE PLAYERS EXPECTED PRAISE AFTER A 7-1 AWAY WIN AT MOLINEUX...
7-0 WOULD HAVE BEEN BETTER. HOW DID THEIR GOAL HAPPEN?
MEANWHILE A NEW WEST STAND WAS BUILT, A WONDERFULLY MODERN CONSTRUCTION WHICH WAS THE ENVY OF ALL OTHER CLUBS. IT COST £45,000, WITH SEATS FOR 4,000 SPECTATORS.
IN 1933 CHAPMAN UNVEILED ARSENAL'S NEW STRIP...
BUT... IT'S GOT **WHITE** SLEEVES!
SO MANY TEAMS PLAY IN COMPLETELY RED SHIRTS, WE HAVE TO BE **DIFFERENT**...
THE BIGGER THEY COME, THE HARDER THEY FALL... IN THE MIDDLE OF THAT SUCCESSFUL SEASON ARSENAL VISITED THIRD DIVISION WALSALL FOR A THIRD ROUND FA CUP TIE.
THEY FELL EXTREMELY HARD!
GILBERT ALSOP GAVE THE MINNOWS A SHOCK LEAD...
THEN...
GOAL!
TAKE THAT!
CAN WE PLAY YOU EVERY WEEK, ARSENAL?
ANOTHER!
OUCH...
WALSALL 2
ARSENAL 0

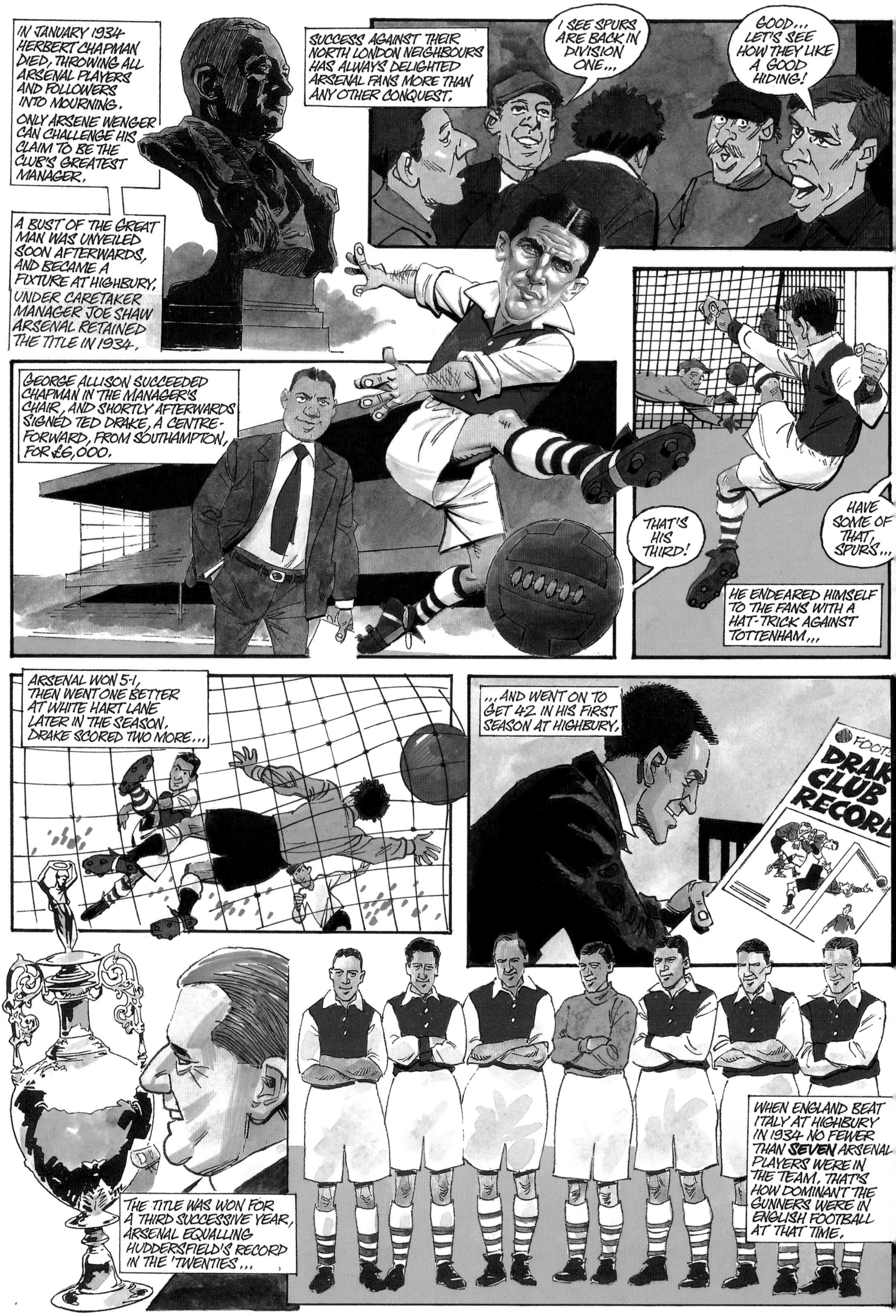
IN JANUARY 1934 HERBERT CHAPMAN DIED, THROWING ALL ARSENAL PLAYERS AND FOLLOWERS INTO MOURNING.
ONLY ARSENE WENGER CAN CHALLENGE HIS CLAIM TO BE THE CLUB'S GREATEST MANAGER.
A BUST OF THE GREAT MAN WAS UNVEILED SOON AFTERWARDS, AND BECAME A FIXTURE AT HIGHBURY.
UNDER CARETAKER MANAGER JOE SHAW ARSENAL RETAINED THE TITLE IN 1934.
SUCCESS AGAINST THEIR NORTH LONDON NEIGHBOURS HAS ALWAYS DELIGHTED ARSENAL FANS MORE THAN ANY OTHER CONQUEST.
I SEE SPURS ARE BACK IN DIVISION ONE...
GOOD... LET'S SEE HOW THEY LIKE A GOOD HIDING!
GEORGE ALLISON SUCCEEDED CHAPMAN IN THE MANAGER'S CHAIR, AND SHORTLY AFTERWARDS SIGNED TED DRAKE, A CENTRE-FORWARD, FROM SOUTHAMPTON, FOR £6,000.
THAT'S HIS THIRD!
HAVE SOME OF THAT, SPURS...
HE ENDEARED HIMSELF TO THE FANS WITH A HAT-TRICK AGAINST TOTTENHAM...
ARSENAL WON 5-1, THEN WENT ONE BETTER AT WHITE HART LANE LATER IN THE SEASON. DRAKE SCORED TWO MORE...
...AND WENT ON TO GET 42 IN HIS FIRST SEASON AT HIGHBURY.
DRAK CLUB RECORD
THE TITLE WAS WON FOR A THIRD SUCCESSIVE YEAR, ARSENAL EQUALLING HUDDERSFIELD'S RECORD IN THE 'TWENTIES...
WHEN ENGLAND BEAT ITALY AT HIGHBURY IN 1934 NO FEWER THAN **SEVEN** ARSENAL PLAYERS WERE IN THE TEAM. THAT'S HOW DOMINANT THE GUNNERS WERE IN ENGLISH FOOTBALL AT THAT TIME.

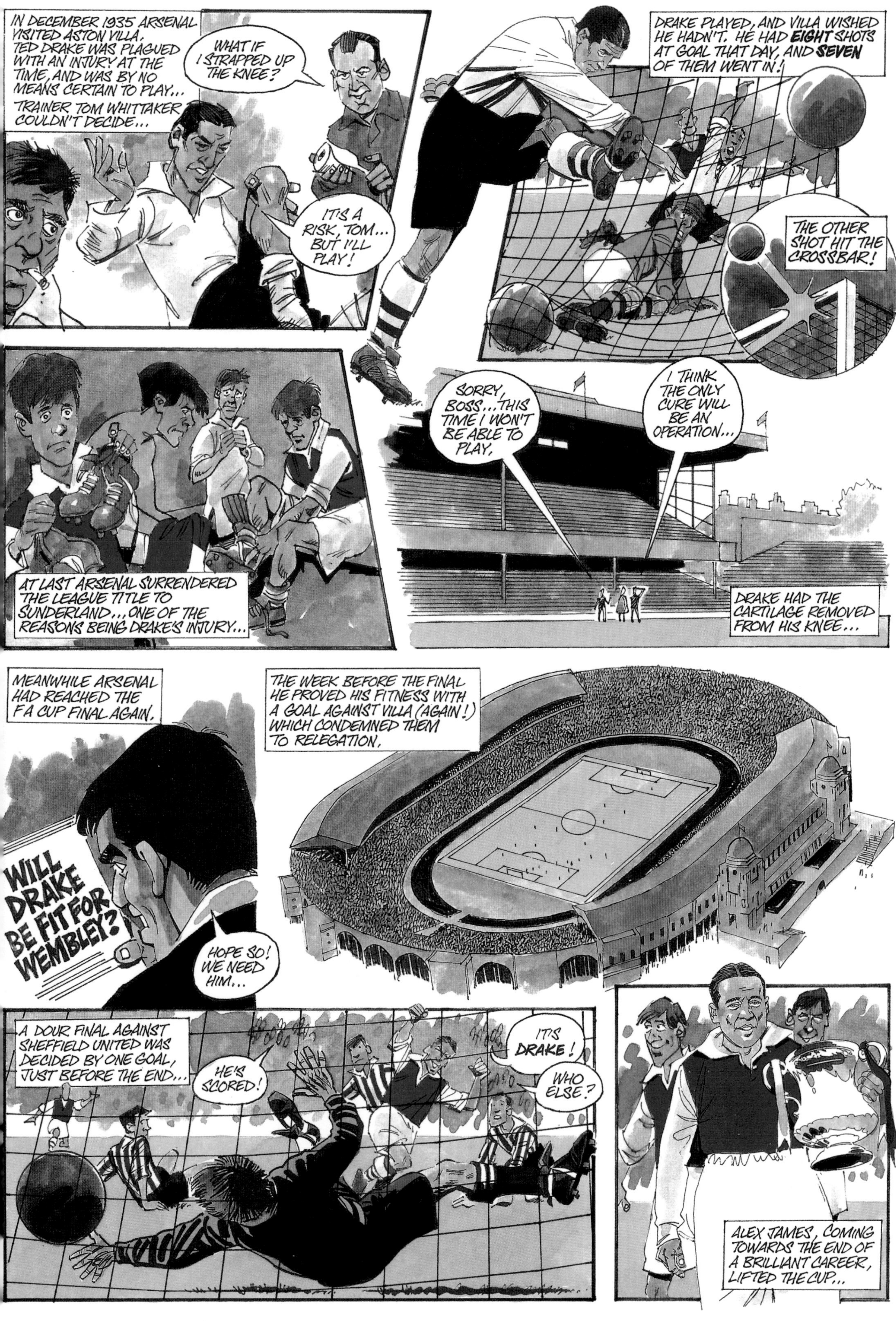
IN DECEMBER 1935 ARSENAL VISITED ASTON VILLA. TED DRAKE WAS PLAGUED WITH AN INJURY AT THE TIME, AND WAS BY NO MEANS CERTAIN TO PLAY...
TRAINER TOM WHITTAKER COULDN'T DECIDE...
WHAT IF I STRAPPED UP THE KNEE?
IT'S A RISK, TOM... BUT I'LL PLAY!
DRAKE PLAYED, AND VILLA WISHED HE HADN'T. HE HAD EIGHT SHOTS AT GOAL THAT DAY, AND SEVEN OF THEM WENT IN!
THE OTHER SHOT HIT THE CROSSBAR!
AT LAST ARSENAL SURRENDERED THE LEAGUE TITLE TO SUNDERLAND... ONE OF THE REASONS BEING DRAKE'S INJURY...
SORRY, BOSS... THIS TIME I WON'T BE ABLE TO PLAY.
I THINK THE ONLY CURE WILL BE AN OPERATION...
DRAKE HAD THE CARTILAGE REMOVED FROM HIS KNEE...
MEANWHILE ARSENAL HAD REACHED THE F A CUP FINAL AGAIN.
WILL DRAKE BE FIT FOR WEMBLEY?
HOPE SO! WE NEED HIM...
THE WEEK BEFORE THE FINAL HE PROVED HIS FITNESS WITH A GOAL AGAINST VILLA (AGAIN!) WHICH CONDEMNED THEM TO RELEGATION.
A DOUR FINAL AGAINST SHEFFIELD UNITED WAS DECIDED BY ONE GOAL, JUST BEFORE THE END...
HE'S SCORED!
IT'S DRAKE!
WHO ELSE?
ALEX JAMES, COMING TOWARDS THE END OF A BRILLIANT CAREER, LIFTED THE CUP...

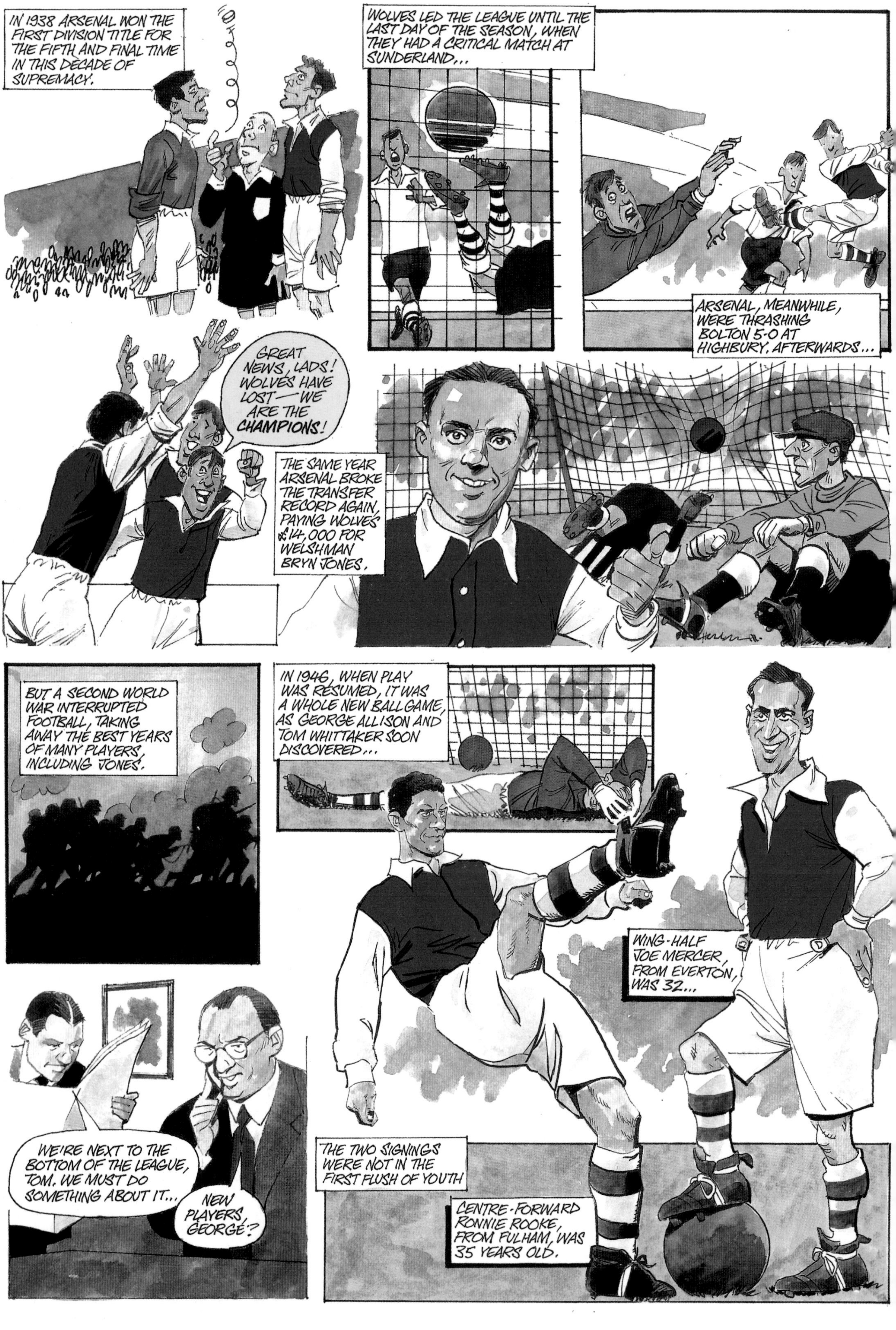
IN 1938 ARSENAL WON THE FIRST DIVISION TITLE FOR THE FIFTH AND FINAL TIME IN THIS DECADE OF SUPREMACY.
WOLVES LED THE LEAGUE UNTIL THE LAST DAY OF THE SEASON, WHEN THEY HAD A CRITICAL MATCH AT SUNDERLAND...
ARSENAL, MEANWHILE, WERE THRASHING BOLTON 5-0 AT HIGHBURY. AFTERWARDS...
GREAT NEWS, LADS! WOLVES HAVE LOST—WE ARE THE CHAMPIONS!
THE SAME YEAR ARSENAL BROKE THE TRANSFER RECORD AGAIN, PAYING WOLVES £14,000 FOR WELSHMAN BRYN JONES.
BUT A SECOND WORLD WAR INTERRUPTED FOOTBALL, TAKING AWAY THE BEST YEARS OF MANY PLAYERS, INCLUDING JONES.
IN 1946, WHEN PLAY WAS RESUMED, IT WAS A WHOLE NEW BALL GAME, AS GEORGE ALLISON AND TOM WHITTAKER SOON DISCOVERED...
WE'RE NEXT TO THE BOTTOM OF THE LEAGUE, TOM. WE MUST DO SOMETHING ABOUT IT...
NEW PLAYERS, GEORGE?
THE TWO SIGNINGS WERE NOT IN THE FIRST FLUSH OF YOUTH
CENTRE-FORWARD RONNIE ROOKE, FROM FULHAM, WAS 35 YEARS OLD.
WING-HALF JOE MERCER, FROM EVERTON, WAS 32...

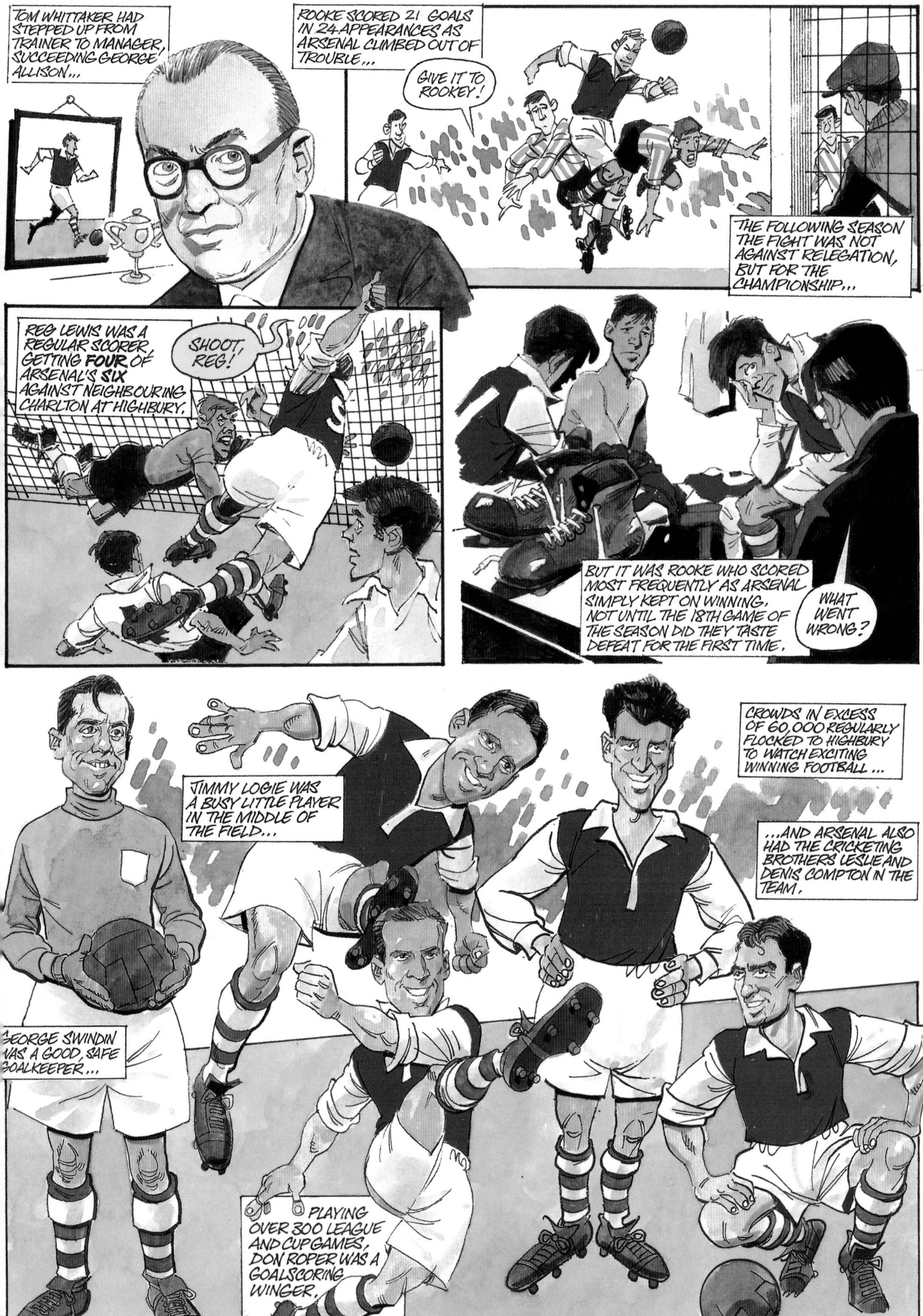
TOM WHITTAKER HAD STEPPED UP FROM TRAINER TO MANAGER, SUCCEEDING GEORGE ALLISON...
ROOKE SCORED 21 GOALS IN 24 APPEARANCES AS ARSENAL CLIMBED OUT OF TROUBLE...
GIVE IT TO ROOKEY!
THE FOLLOWING SEASON THE FIGHT WAS NOT AGAINST RELEGATION, BUT FOR THE CHAMPIONSHIP...
REG LEWIS WAS A REGULAR SCORER, GETTING **FOUR** OF ARSENAL'S **SIX** AGAINST NEIGHBOURING CHARLTON AT HIGHBURY.
SHOOT, REG!
BUT IT WAS ROOKE WHO SCORED MOST FREQUENTLY AS ARSENAL SIMPLY KEPT ON WINNING. NOT UNTIL THE 18TH GAME OF THE SEASON DID THEY TASTE DEFEAT FOR THE FIRST TIME.
WHAT WENT WRONG?
GEORGE SWINDIN WAS A GOOD, SAFE GOALKEEPER...
JIMMY LOGIE WAS A BUSY LITTLE PLAYER IN THE MIDDLE OF THE FIELD...
PLAYING OVER 300 LEAGUE AND CUP GAMES, DON ROPER WAS A GOALSCORING WINGER.
CROWDS IN EXCESS OF 60,000 REGULARLY FLOCKED TO HIGHBURY TO WATCH EXCITING WINNING FOOTBALL...
...AND ARSENAL ALSO HAD THE CRICKETING BROTHERS LESLIE AND DENIS COMPTON IN THE TEAM.

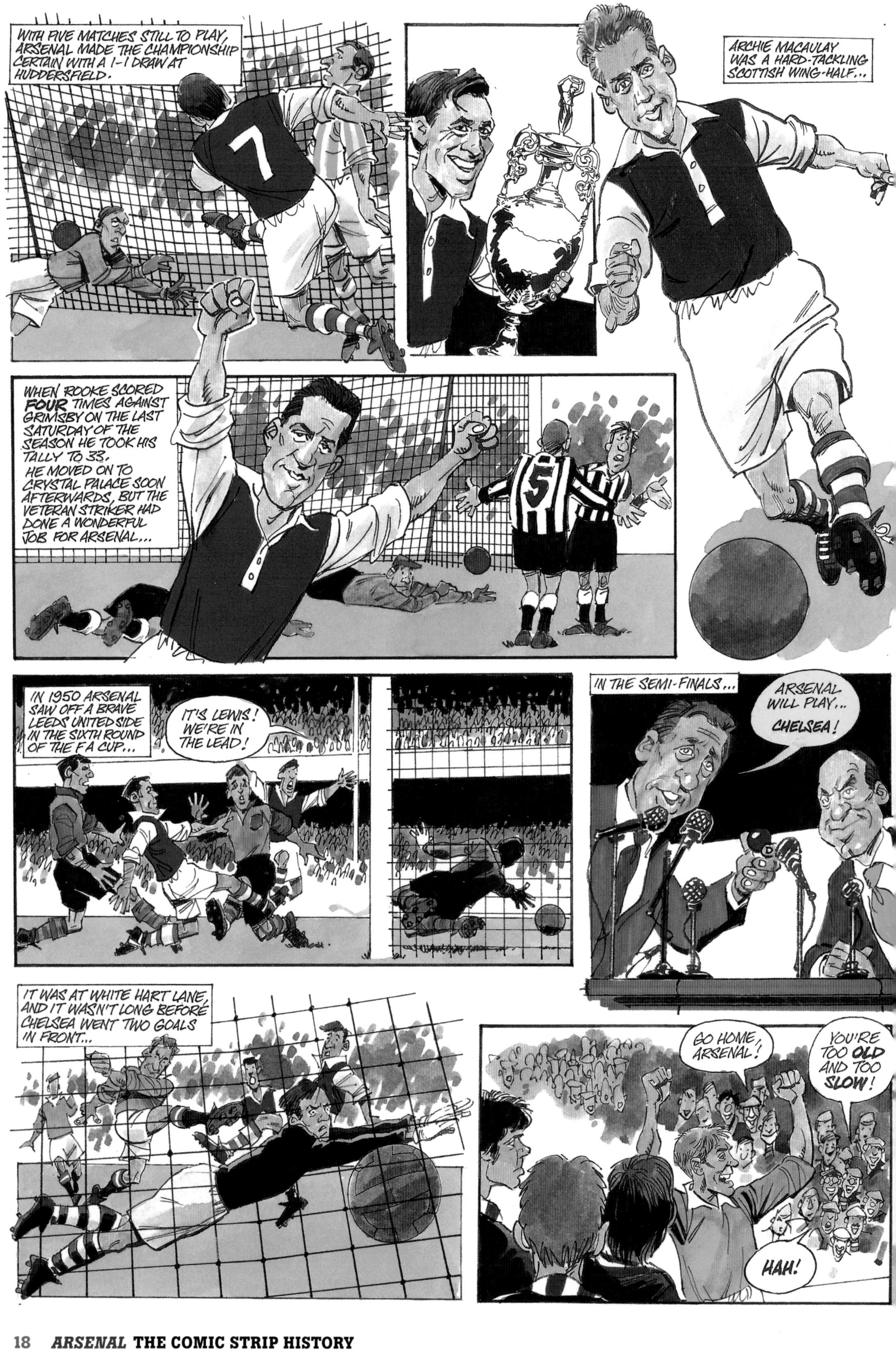

WITH FIVE MATCHES STILL TO PLAY, ARSENAL MADE THE CHAMPIONSHIP CERTAIN WITH A 1-1 DRAW AT HUDDERSFIELD.
ARCHIE MACAULAY WAS A HARD-TACKLING SCOTTISH WING-HALF...
WHEN ROOKE SCORED FOUR TIMES AGAINST GRIMSBY ON THE LAST SATURDAY OF THE SEASON HE TOOK HIS TALLY TO 33. HE MOVED ON TO CRYSTAL PALACE SOON AFTERWARDS, BUT THE VETERAN STRIKER HAD DONE A WONDERFUL JOB FOR ARSENAL...
IN 1950 ARSENAL SAW OFF A BRAVE LEEDS UNITED SIDE IN THE SIXTH ROUND OF THE F A CUP...
IT'S LEWIS! WE'RE IN THE LEAD!
IN THE SEMI-FINALS...
ARSENAL WILL PLAY... CHELSEA!
IT WAS AT WHITE HART LANE, AND IT WASN'T LONG BEFORE CHELSEA WENT TWO GOALS IN FRONT...
GO HOME, ARSENAL!
YOU'RE TOO OLD AND TOO SLOW!
HAH!

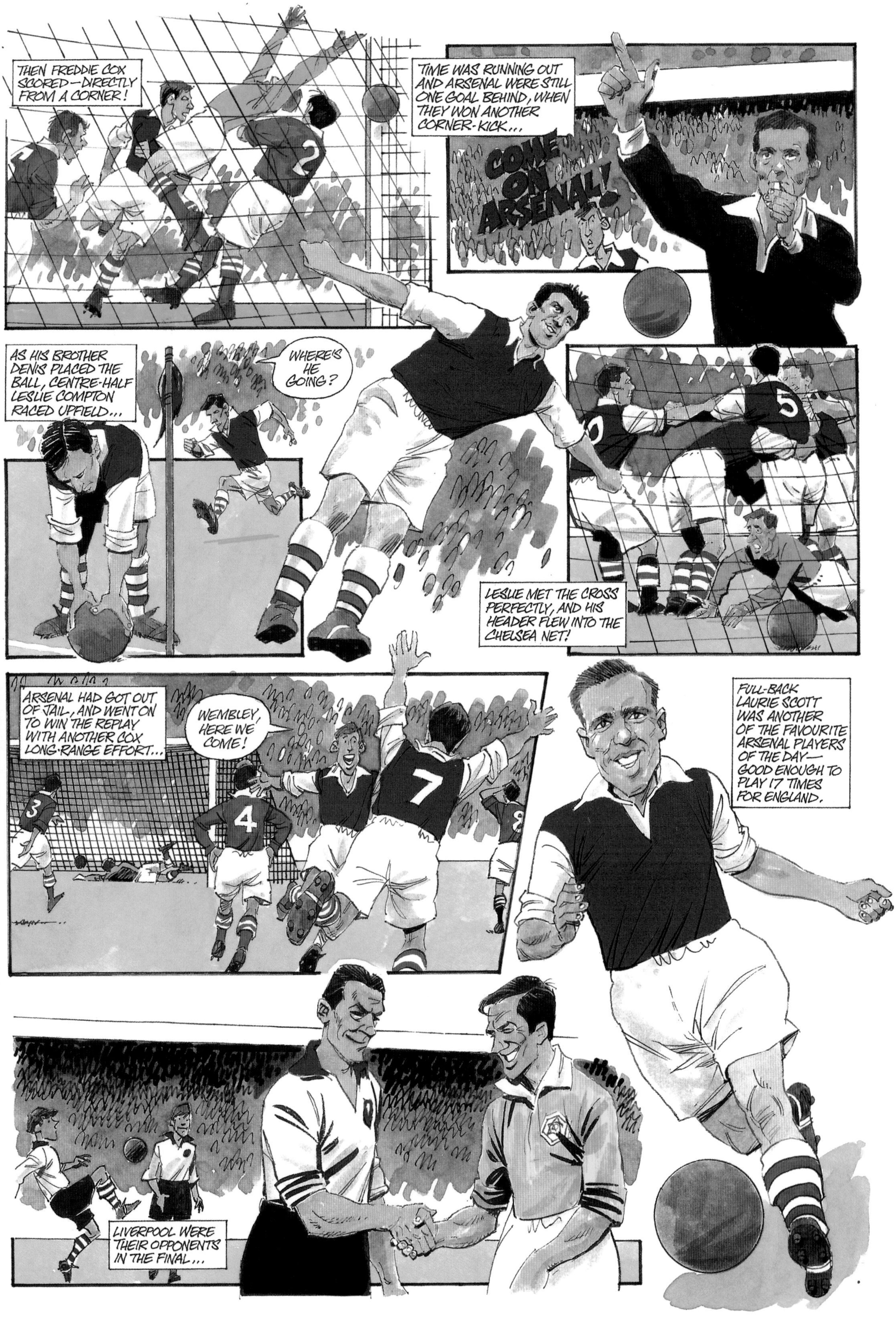
THEN FREDDIE COX SCORED—DIRECTLY FROM A CORNER!
TIME WAS RUNNING OUT AND ARSENAL WERE STILL ONE GOAL BEHIND, WHEN THEY WON ANOTHER CORNER-KICK...
COME ON ARSENAL!
AS HIS BROTHER DENIS PLACED THE BALL, CENTRE-HALF LESLIE COMPTON RACED UPFIELD...
WHERE'S HE GOING?
LESLIE MET THE CROSS PERFECTLY, AND HIS HEADER FLEW INTO THE CHELSEA NET!
ARSENAL HAD GOT OUT OF JAIL, AND WENT ON TO WIN THE REPLAY WITH ANOTHER COX LONG-RANGE EFFORT...
WEMBLEY, HERE WE COME!
FULL-BACK LAURIE SCOTT WAS ANOTHER OF THE FAVOURITE ARSENAL PLAYERS OF THE DAY—GOOD ENOUGH TO PLAY 17 TIMES FOR ENGLAND.
LIVERPOOL WERE THEIR OPPONENTS IN THE FINAL...

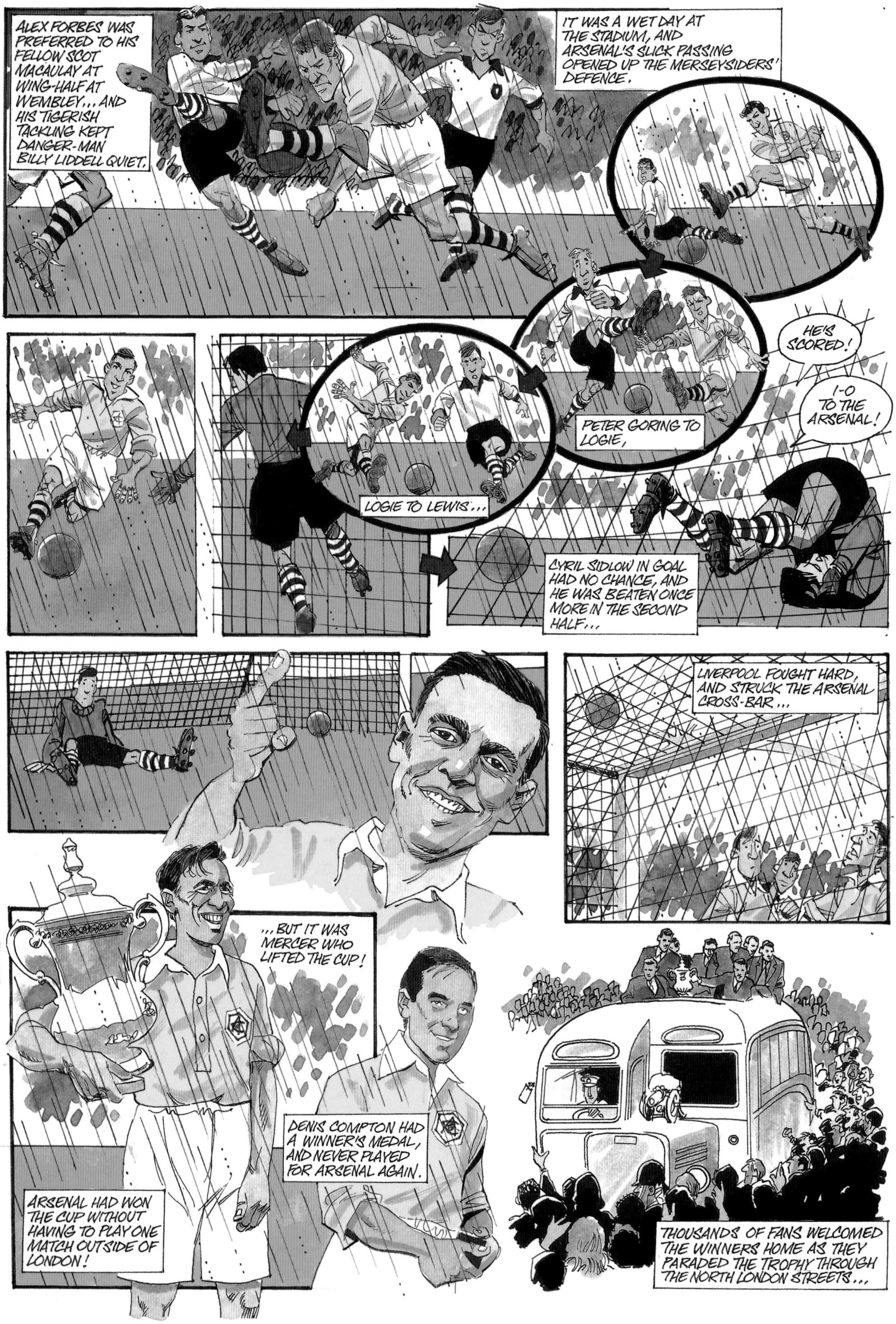
ALEX FORBES WAS PREFERRED TO HIS FELLOW SCOT MACAULAY AT WING-HALF AT WEMBLEY... AND HIS TIGERISH TACKLING KEPT DANGER-MAN BILLY LIDDELL QUIET.
IT WAS A WET DAY AT THE STADIUM, AND ARSENAL'S SLICK PASSING OPENED UP THE MERSEYSIDERS' DEFENCE.
PETER GORING TO LOGIE,
LOGIE TO LEWIS...
HE'S SCORED!
1-0 TO THE ARSENAL!
CYRIL SIDLOW IN GOAL HAD NO CHANCE, AND HE WAS BEATEN ONCE MORE IN THE SECOND HALF...
LIVERPOOL FOUGHT HARD, AND STRUCK THE ARSENAL CROSS-BAR...
...BUT IT WAS MERCER WHO LIFTED THE CUP!
DENIS COMPTON HAD A WINNER'S MEDAL, AND NEVER PLAYED FOR ARSENAL AGAIN.
ARSENAL HAD WON THE CUP WITHOUT HAVING TO PLAY ONE MATCH OUTSIDE OF LONDON!
THOUSANDS OF FANS WELCOMED THE WINNERS HOME AS THEY PARADED THE TROPHY THROUGH THE NORTH LONDON STREETS...

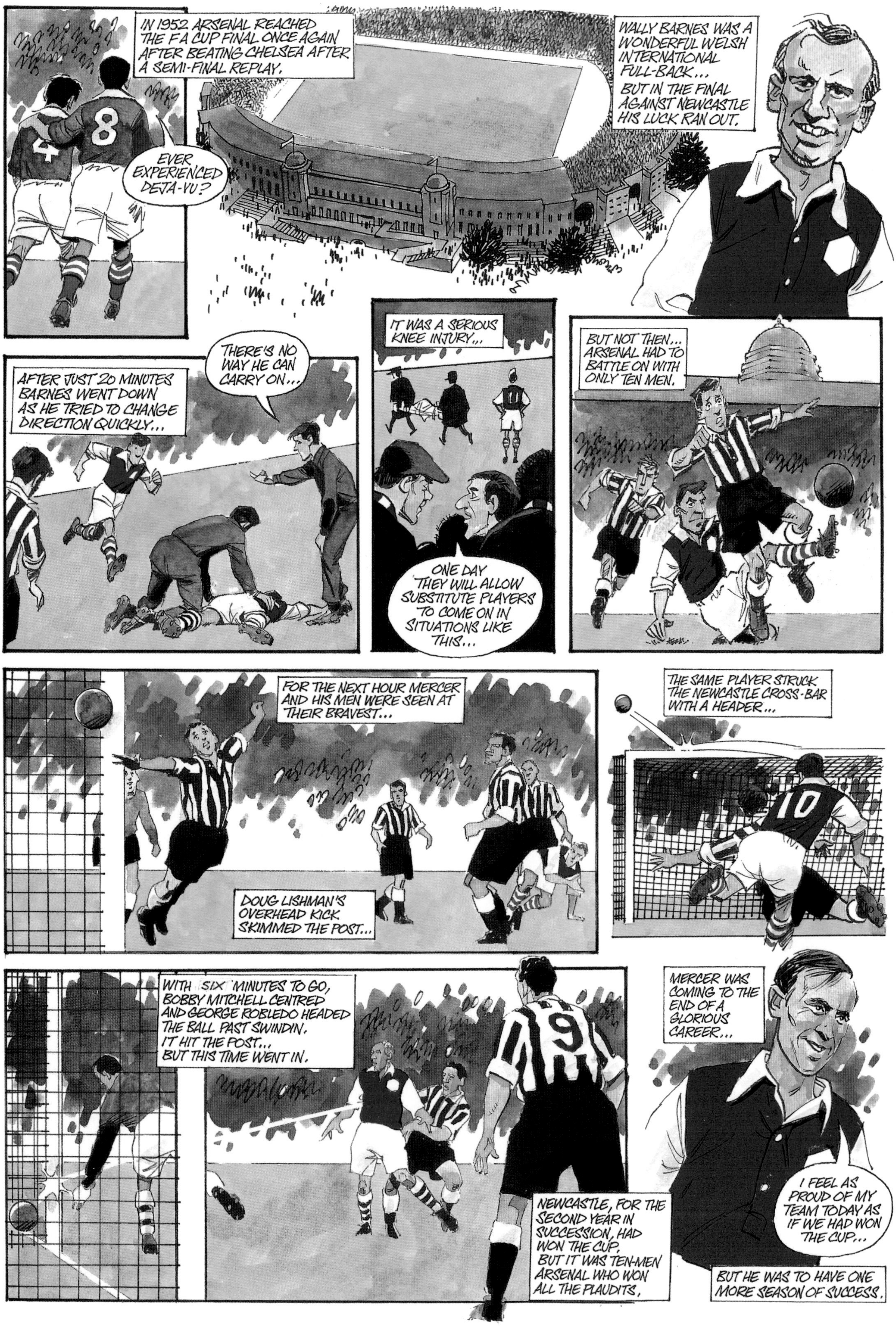
IN 1952 ARSENAL REACHED THE F A CUP FINAL ONCE AGAIN AFTER BEATING CHELSEA AFTER A SEMI-FINAL REPLAY.
EVER EXPERIENCED DEJA-VU?
WALLY BARNES WAS A WONDERFUL WELSH INTERNATIONAL FULL-BACK...
BUT IN THE FINAL AGAINST NEWCASTLE HIS LUCK RAN OUT.
AFTER JUST 20 MINUTES BARNES WENT DOWN AS HE TRIED TO CHANGE DIRECTION QUICKLY...
THERE'S NO WAY HE CAN CARRY ON...
IT WAS A SERIOUS KNEE INJURY...
ONE DAY THEY WILL ALLOW SUBSTITUTE PLAYERS TO COME ON IN SITUATIONS LIKE THIS...
BUT NOT THEN... ARSENAL HAD TO BATTLE ON WITH ONLY TEN MEN.
FOR THE NEXT HOUR MERCER AND HIS MEN WERE SEEN AT THEIR BRAVEST...
DOUG LISHMAN'S OVERHEAD KICK SKIMMED THE POST...
THE SAME PLAYER STRUCK THE NEWCASTLE CROSS-BAR WITH A HEADER...
WITH SIX MINUTES TO GO, BOBBY MITCHELL CENTRED AND GEORGE ROBLEDO HEADED THE BALL PAST SWINDIN. IT HIT THE POST... BUT THIS TIME WENT IN.
NEWCASTLE, FOR THE SECOND YEAR IN SUCCESSION, HAD WON THE CUP. BUT IT WAS TEN-MEN ARSENAL WHO WON ALL THE PLAUDITS.
MERCER WAS COMING TO THE END OF A GLORIOUS CAREER...
I FEEL AS PROUD OF MY TEAM TODAY AS IF WE HAD WON THE CUP...
BUT HE WAS TO HAVE ONE MORE SEASON OF SUCCESS.

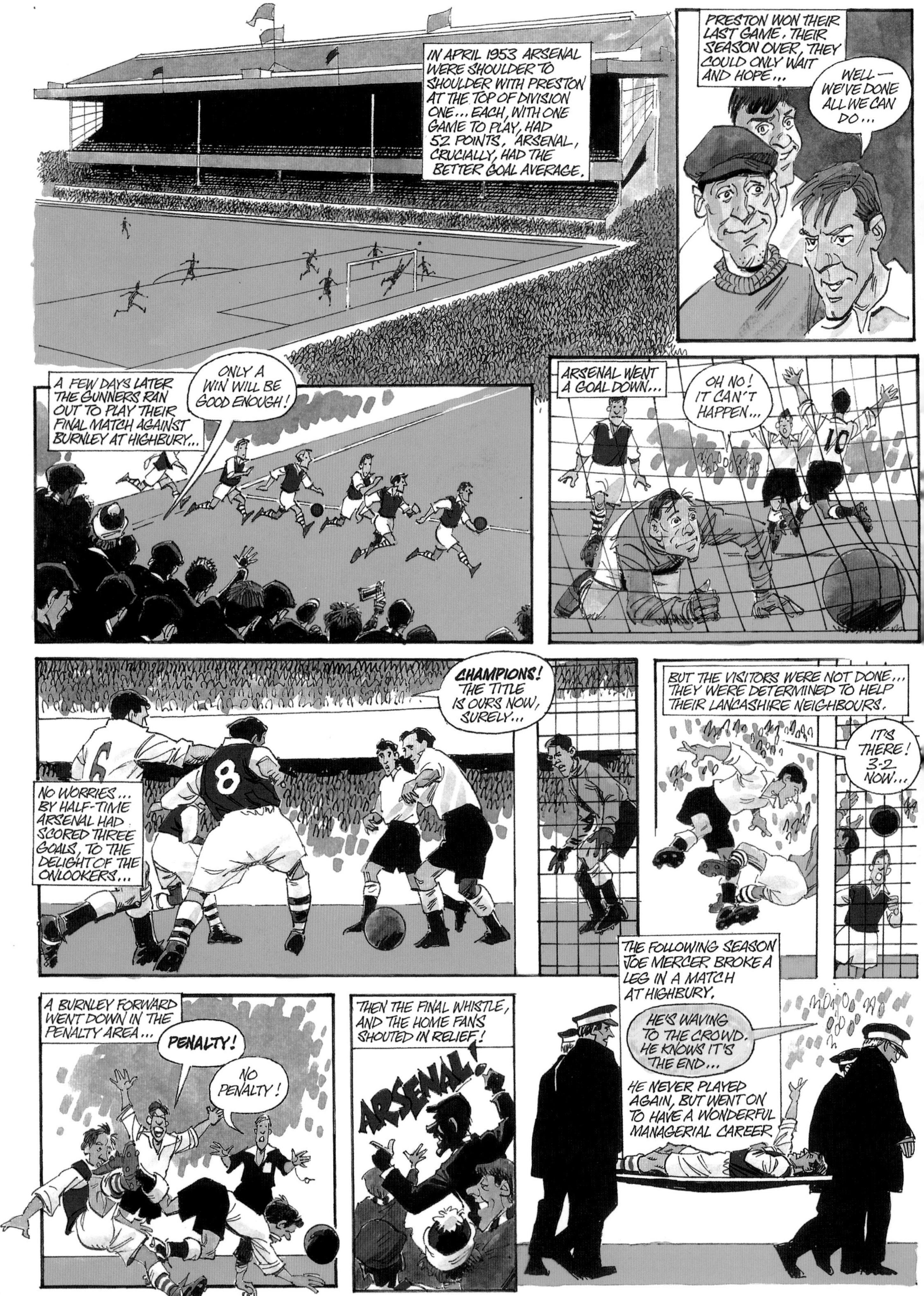
IN APRIL 1953 ARSENAL WERE SHOULDER TO SHOULDER WITH PRESTON AT THE TOP OF DIVISION ONE... EACH, WITH ONE GAME TO PLAY, HAD 52 POINTS. ARSENAL, CRUCIALLY, HAD THE BETTER GOAL AVERAGE.
PRESTON WON THEIR LAST GAME, THEIR SEASON OVER, THEY COULD ONLY WAIT AND HOPE...
WELL — WE'VE DONE ALL WE CAN DO...
A FEW DAYS LATER THE GUNNERS RAN OUT TO PLAY THEIR FINAL MATCH AGAINST BURNLEY AT HIGHBURY...
ONLY A WIN WILL BE GOOD ENOUGH!
ARSENAL WENT A GOAL DOWN...
OH NO! IT CAN'T HAPPEN...
CHAMPIONS! THE TITLE IS OURS NOW, SURELY...
NO WORRIES... BY HALF-TIME ARSENAL HAD SCORED THREE GOALS, TO THE DELIGHT OF THE ONLOOKERS...
BUT THE VISITORS WERE NOT DONE... THEY WERE DETERMINED TO HELP THEIR LANCASHIRE NEIGHBOURS.
IT'S THERE! 3-2 NOW...
A BURNLEY FORWARD WENT DOWN IN THE PENALTY AREA...
PENALTY!
NO PENALTY!
THEN THE FINAL WHISTLE, AND THE HOME FANS SHOUTED IN RELIEF!
ARSENAL!
THE FOLLOWING SEASON JOE MERCER BROKE A LEG IN A MATCH AT HIGHBURY.
HE'S WAVING TO THE CROWD. HE KNOWS IT'S THE END...
HE NEVER PLAYED AGAIN, BUT WENT ON TO HAVE A WONDERFUL MANAGERIAL CAREER

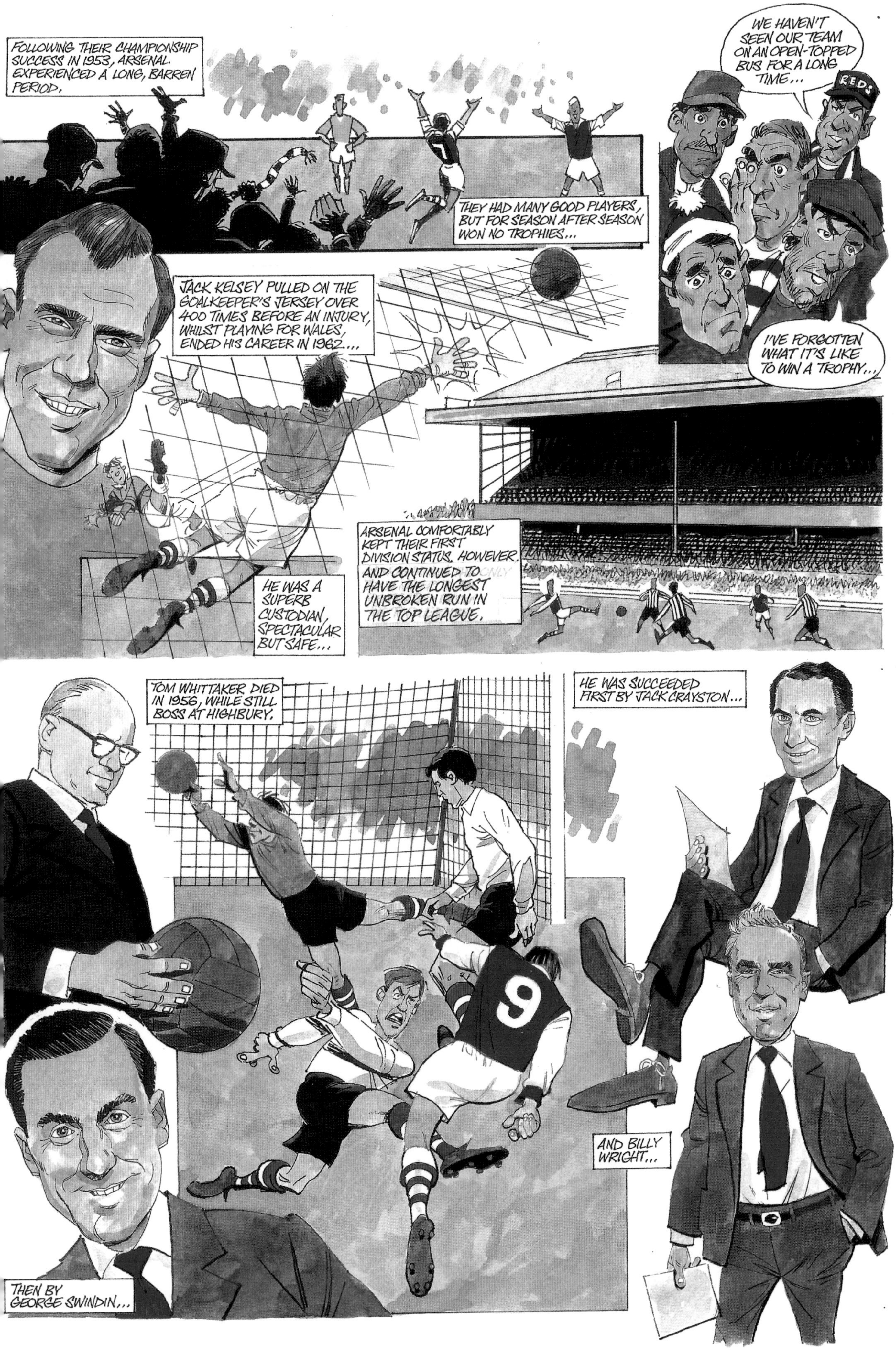
FOLLOWING THEIR CHAMPIONSHIP SUCCESS IN 1953, ARSENAL EXPERIENCED A LONG, BARREN PERIOD,
THEY HAD MANY GOOD PLAYERS, BUT FOR SEASON AFTER SEASON WON NO TROPHIES...
WE HAVEN'T SEEN OUR TEAM ON AN OPEN-TOPPED BUS FOR A LONG TIME...
REDS
I'VE FORGOTTEN WHAT IT'S LIKE TO WIN A TROPHY...
JACK KELSEY PULLED ON THE GOALKEEPER'S JERSEY OVER 400 TIMES BEFORE AN INJURY, WHILST PLAYING FOR WALES, ENDED HIS CAREER IN 1962...
HE WAS A SUPERB CUSTODIAN, SPECTACULAR BUT SAFE...
ARSENAL COMFORTABLY KEPT THEIR FIRST DIVISION STATUS, HOWEVER, AND CONTINUED TO HAVE THE LONGEST UNBROKEN RUN IN THE TOP LEAGUE.
TOM WHITTAKER DIED IN 1956, WHILE STILL BOSS AT HIGHBURY.
HE WAS SUCCEEDED FIRST BY JACK CRAYSTON...
9
THEN BY GEORGE SWINDIN...
AND BILLY WRIGHT...

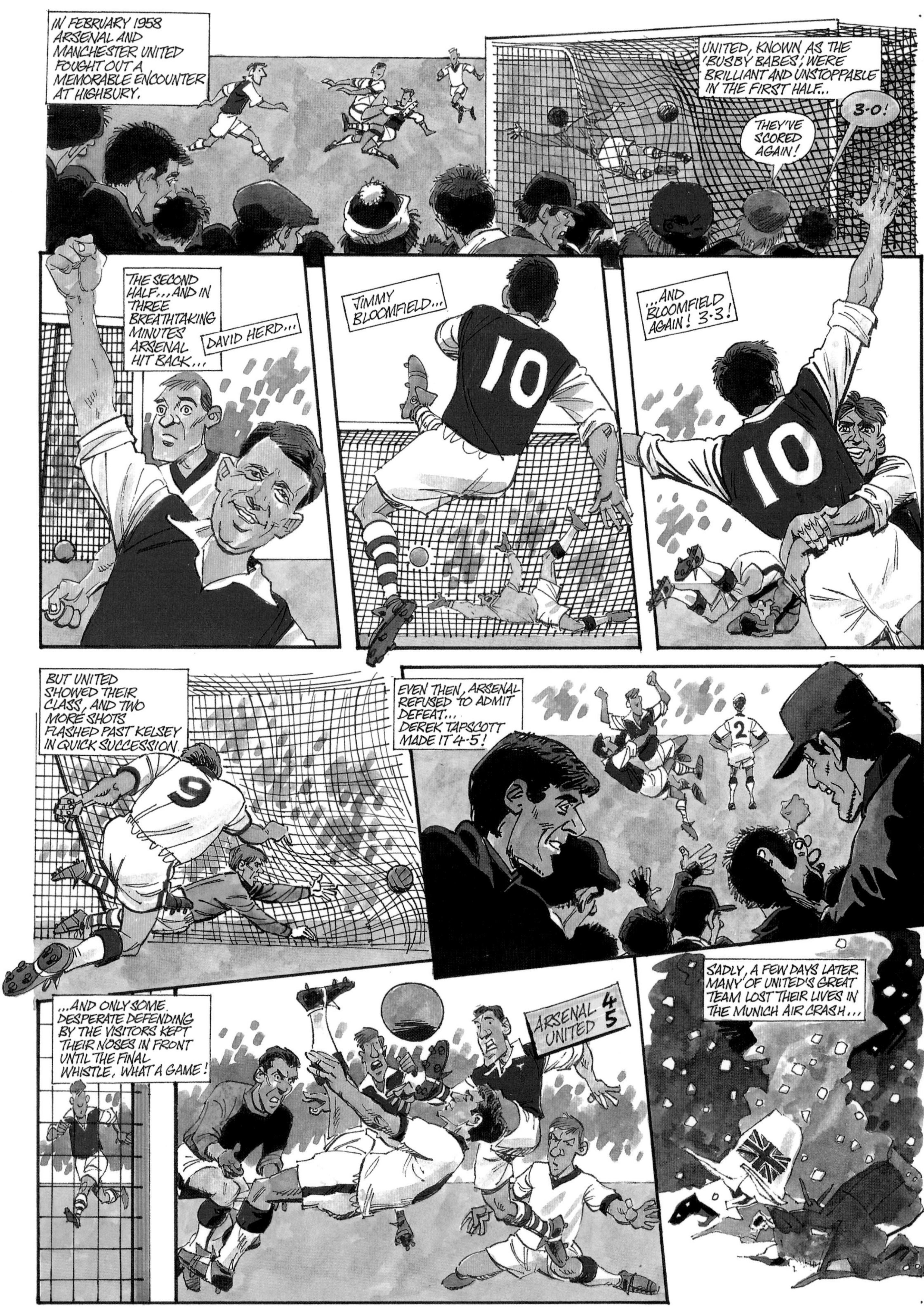
IN FEBRUARY 1958 ARSENAL AND MANCHESTER UNITED FOUGHT OUT A MEMORABLE ENCOUNTER AT HIGHBURY.
UNITED, KNOWN AS THE 'BUSBY BABES', WERE BRILLIANT AND UNSTOPPABLE IN THE FIRST HALF...
THEY'VE SCORED AGAIN!
3-0!
THE SECOND HALF... AND IN THREE BREATHTAKING MINUTES ARSENAL HIT BACK...
DAVID HERD...
JIMMY BLOOMFIELD...
...AND BLOOMFIELD AGAIN! 3-3!
BUT UNITED SHOWED THEIR CLASS, AND TWO MORE SHOTS FLASHED PAST KELSEY IN QUICK SUCCESSION.
EVEN THEN, ARSENAL REFUSED TO ADMIT DEFEAT... DEREK TAPSCOTT MADE IT 4-5!
...AND ONLY SOME DESPERATE DEFENDING BY THE VISITORS KEPT THEIR NOSES IN FRONT UNTIL THE FINAL WHISTLE. WHAT A GAME!
ARSENAL 4
UNITED 5
SADLY, A FEW DAYS LATER MANY OF UNITED'S GREAT TEAM LOST THEIR LIVES IN THE MUNICH AIR CRASH...

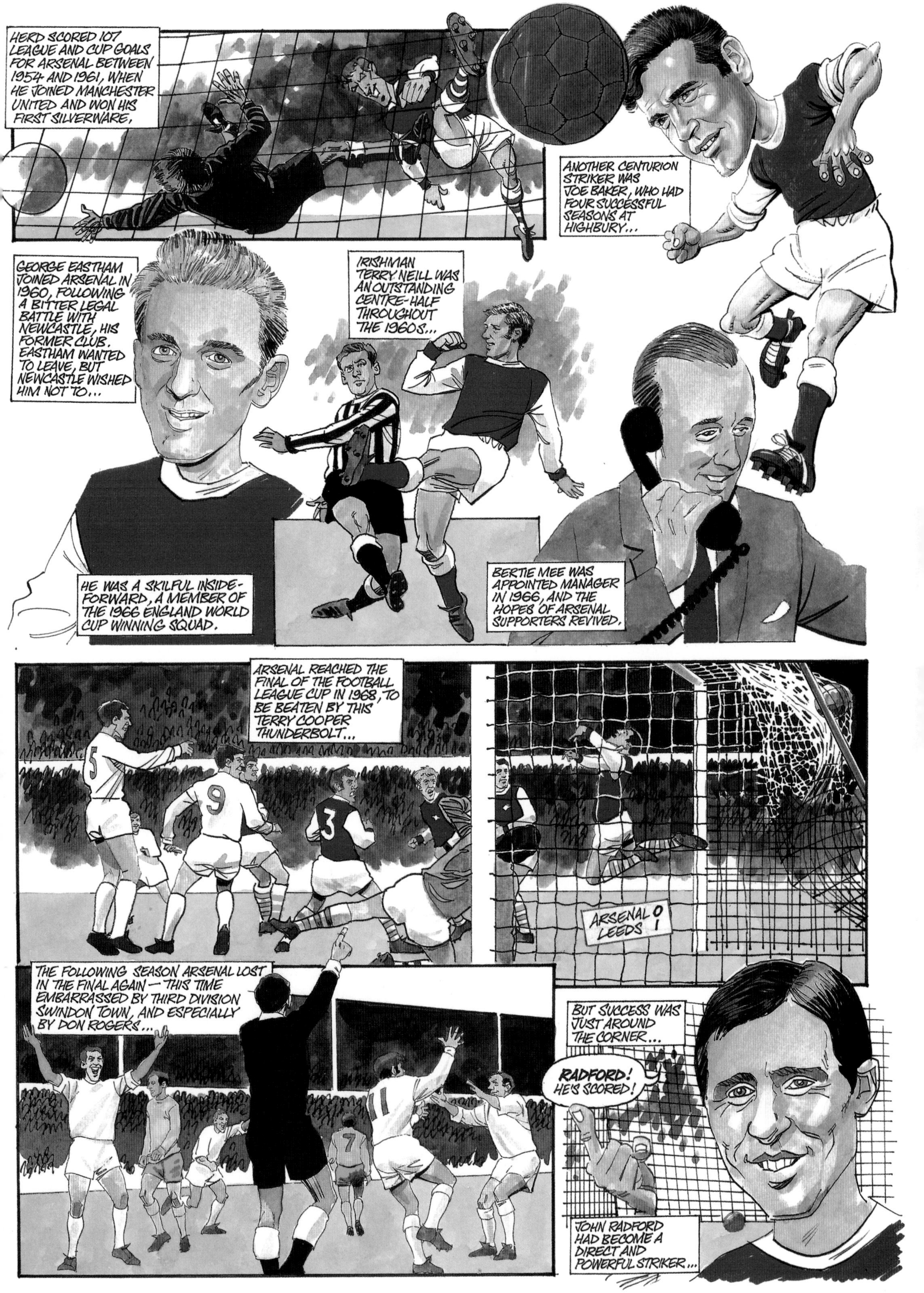
HERD SCORED 107 LEAGUE AND CUP GOALS FOR ARSENAL BETWEEN 1954 AND 1961, WHEN HE JOINED MANCHESTER UNITED AND WON HIS FIRST SILVERWARE.
ANOTHER CENTURION STRIKER WAS JOE BAKER, WHO HAD FOUR SUCCESSFUL SEASONS AT HIGHBURY...
GEORGE EASTHAM JOINED ARSENAL IN 1960, FOLLOWING A BITTER LEGAL BATTLE WITH NEWCASTLE, HIS FORMER CLUB. EASTHAM WANTED TO LEAVE, BUT NEWCASTLE WISHED HIM NOT TO...
HE WAS A SKILFUL INSIDE-FORWARD, A MEMBER OF THE 1966 ENGLAND WORLD CUP WINNING SQUAD.
IRISHMAN TERRY NEILL WAS AN OUTSTANDING CENTRE-HALF THROUGHOUT THE 1960S...
BERTIE MEE WAS APPOINTED MANAGER IN 1966, AND THE HOPES OF ARSENAL SUPPORTERS REVIVED.
ARSENAL REACHED THE FINAL OF THE FOOTBALL LEAGUE CUP IN 1968, TO BE BEATEN BY THIS TERRY COOPER THUNDERBOLT...
ARSENAL 0
LEEDS 1
THE FOLLOWING SEASON ARSENAL LOST IN THE FINAL AGAIN — THIS TIME EMBARRASSED BY THIRD DIVISION SWINDON TOWN, AND ESPECIALLY BY DON ROGERS...
BUT SUCCESS WAS JUST AROUND THE CORNER...
RADFORD! HE'S SCORED!
JOHN RADFORD HAD BECOME A DIRECT AND POWERFUL STRIKER...

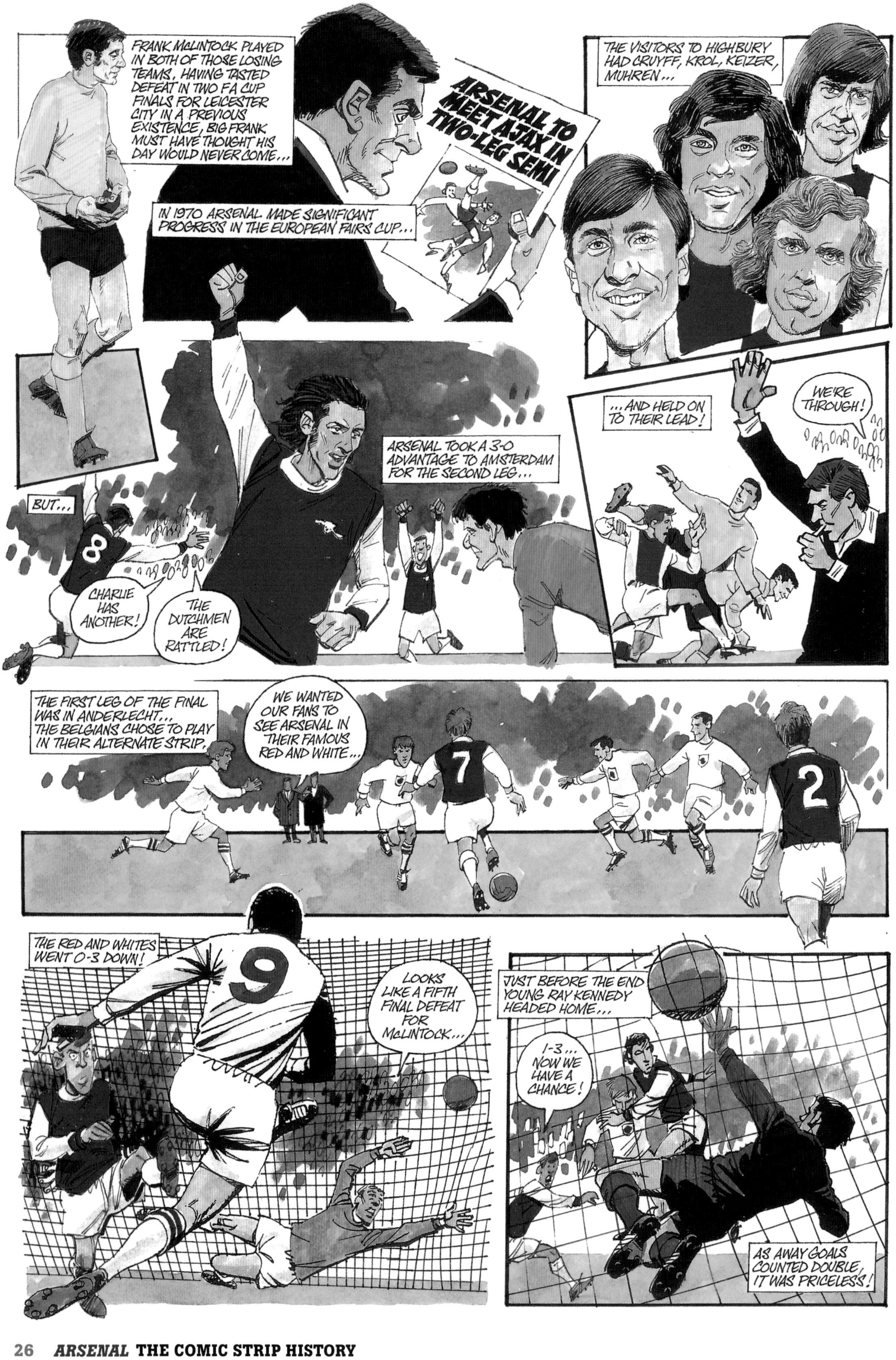

FRANK McLINTOCK PLAYED IN BOTH OF THOSE LOSING TEAMS, HAVING TASTED DEFEAT IN TWO FA CUP FINALS FOR LEICESTER CITY IN A PREVIOUS EXISTENCE, BIG FRANK MUST HAVE THOUGHT HIS DAY WOULD NEVER COME...
ARSENAL TO MEET AJAX IN TWO-LEG SEMI
IN 1970 ARSENAL MADE SIGNIFICANT PROGRESS IN THE EUROPEAN FAIRS CUP...
THE VISITORS TO HIGHBURY HAD CRUYFF, KROL, KEIZER, MUHREN...
BUT...
CHARLIE HAS ANOTHER!
THE DUTCHMEN ARE RATTLED!
ARSENAL TOOK A 3-0 ADVANTAGE TO AMSTERDAM FOR THE SECOND LEG...
...AND HELD ON TO THEIR LEAD!
WE'RE THROUGH!
THE FIRST LEG OF THE FINAL WAS IN ANDERLECHT... THE BELGIANS CHOSE TO PLAY IN THEIR ALTERNATE STRIP.
WE WANTED OUR FANS TO SEE ARSENAL IN THEIR FAMOUS RED AND WHITE...
THE RED AND WHITES WENT 0-3 DOWN!
LOOKS LIKE A FIFTH FINAL DEFEAT FOR McLINTOCK...
JUST BEFORE THE END YOUNG RAY KENNEDY HEADED HOME...
1-3... NOW WE HAVE A CHANCE!
AS AWAY GOALS COUNTED DOUBLE, IT WAS PRICELESS!

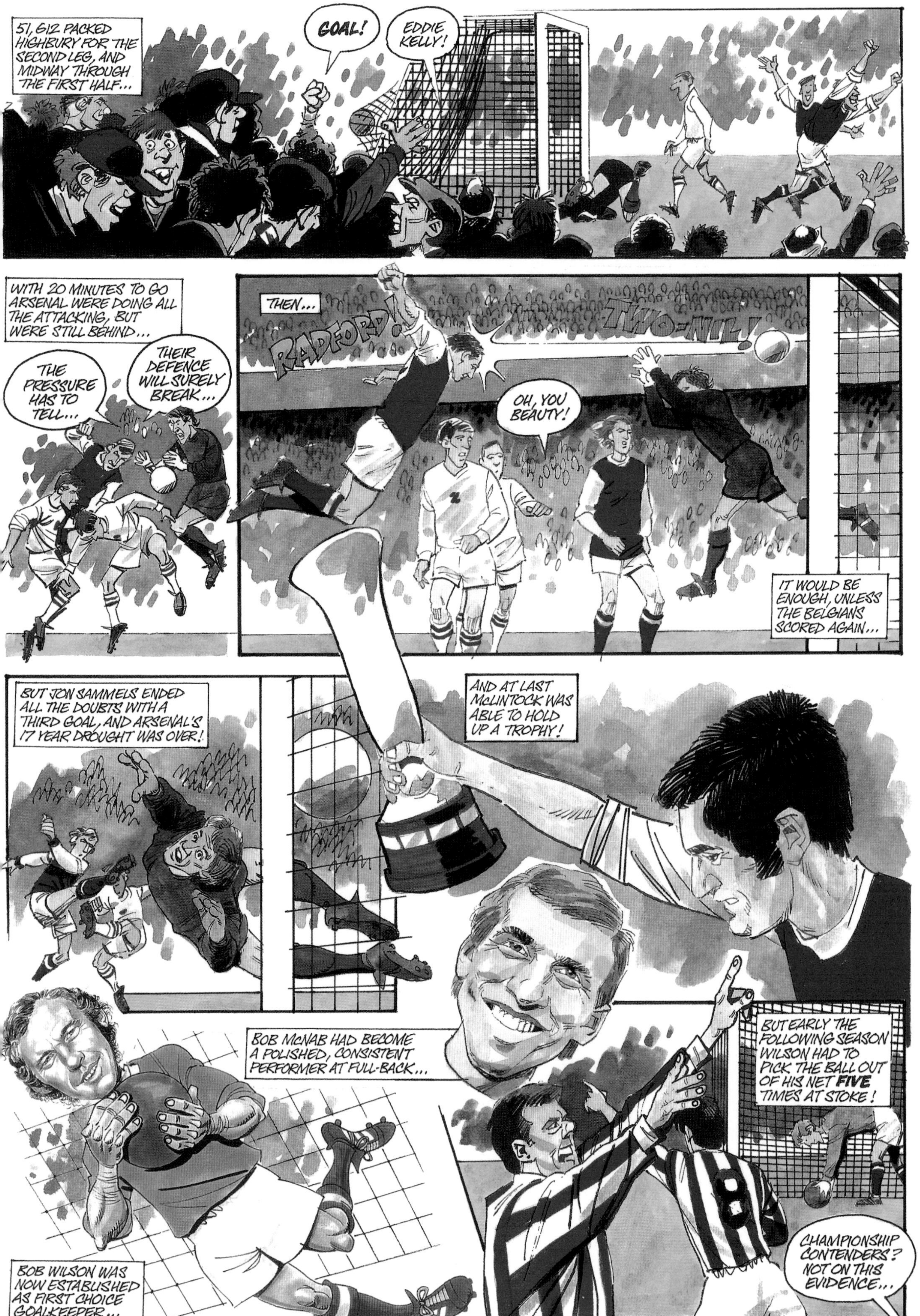

51,612 PACKED HIGHBURY FOR THE SECOND LEG, AND MIDWAY THROUGH THE FIRST HALF...
GOAL!
EDDIE KELLY!
WITH 20 MINUTES TO GO ARSENAL WERE DOING ALL THE ATTACKING, BUT WERE STILL BEHIND...
THE PRESSURE HAS TO TELL...
THEIR DEFENCE WILL SURELY BREAK...
THEN...
RADFORD!
TWO-NIL!
OH, YOU BEAUTY!
IT WOULD BE ENOUGH, UNLESS THE BELGIANS SCORED AGAIN...
BUT JON SAMMELS ENDED ALL THE DOUBTS WITH A THIRD GOAL, AND ARSENAL'S 17 YEAR DROUGHT WAS OVER!
AND AT LAST McLINTOCK WAS ABLE TO HOLD UP A TROPHY!
BOB McNAB HAD BECOME A POLISHED, CONSISTENT PERFORMER AT FULL-BACK...
BUT EARLY THE FOLLOWING SEASON WILSON HAD TO PICK THE BALL OUT OF HIS NET **FIVE** TIMES AT STOKE!
BOB WILSON WAS NOW ESTABLISHED AS FIRST CHOICE GOALKEEPER...
CHAMPIONSHIP CONTENDERS? NOT ON THIS EVIDENCE...

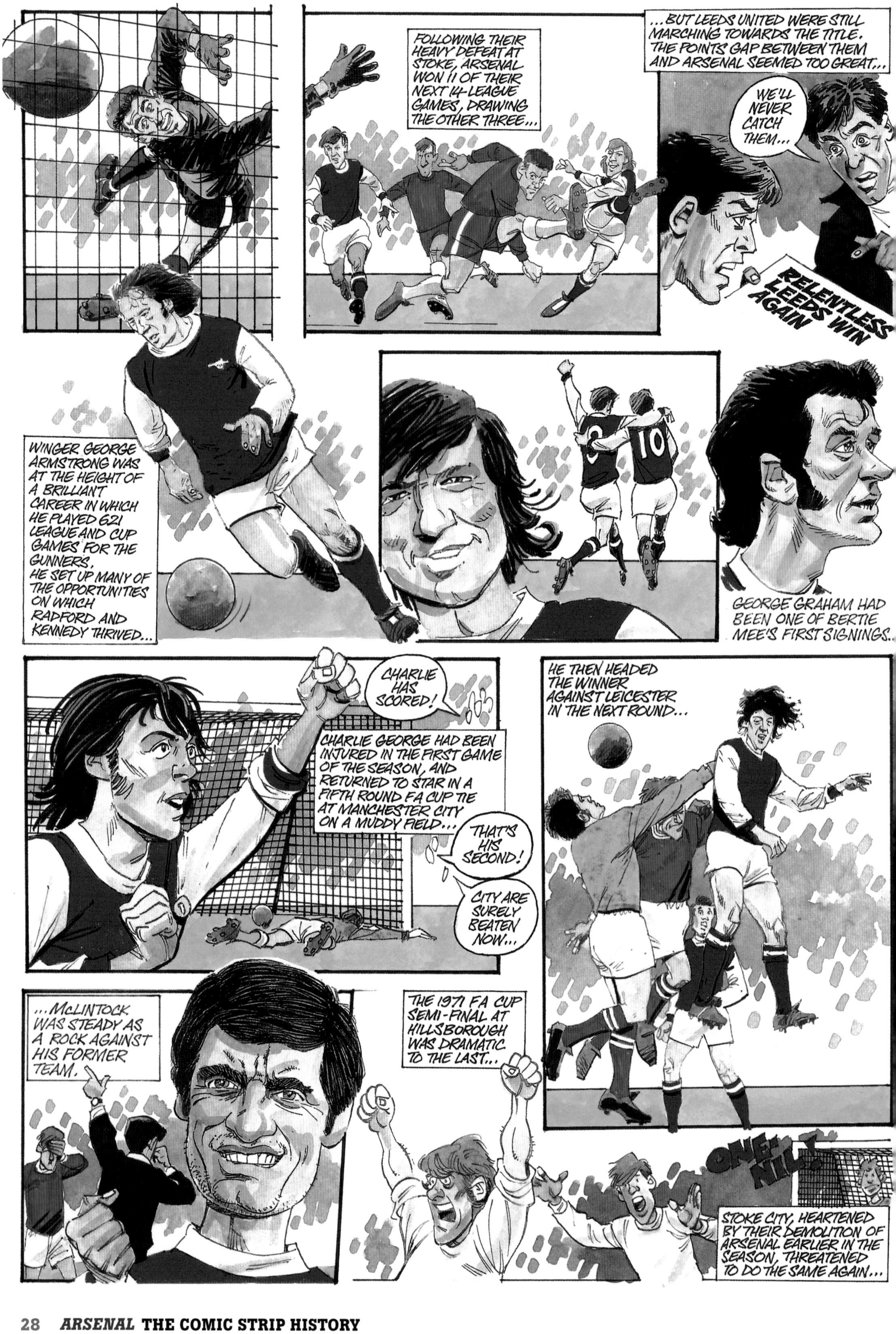
FOLLOWING THEIR HEAVY DEFEAT AT STOKE, ARSENAL WON 11 OF THEIR NEXT 14 LEAGUE GAMES, DRAWING THE OTHER THREE...
...BUT LEEDS UNITED WERE STILL MARCHING TOWARDS THE TITLE. THE POINTS GAP BETWEEN THEM AND ARSENAL SEEMED TOO GREAT...
WE'LL NEVER CATCH THEM...
RELENTLESS LEEDS WIN AGAIN
WINGER GEORGE ARMSTRONG WAS AT THE HEIGHT OF A BRILLIANT CAREER IN WHICH HE PLAYED 621 LEAGUE AND CUP GAMES FOR THE GUNNERS. HE SET UP MANY OF THE OPPORTUNITIES ON WHICH RADFORD AND KENNEDY THRIVED...
GEORGE GRAHAM HAD BEEN ONE OF BERTIE MEE'S FIRST SIGNINGS...
CHARLIE HAS SCORED!
CHARLIE GEORGE HAD BEEN INJURED IN THE FIRST GAME OF THE SEASON, AND RETURNED TO STAR IN A FIFTH ROUND FA CUP TIE AT MANCHESTER CITY ON A MUDDY FIELD...
THAT'S HIS SECOND!
CITY ARE SURELY BEATEN NOW...
HE THEN HEADED THE WINNER AGAINST LEICESTER IN THE NEXT ROUND...
...McLINTOCK WAS STEADY AS A ROCK AGAINST HIS FORMER TEAM.
THE 1971 FA CUP SEMI-FINAL AT HILLSBOROUGH WAS DRAMATIC TO THE LAST...
ONE-NIL!
STOKE CITY, HEARTENED BY THEIR DEMOLITION OF ARSENAL EARLIER IN THE SEASON, THREATENED TO DO THE SAME AGAIN...

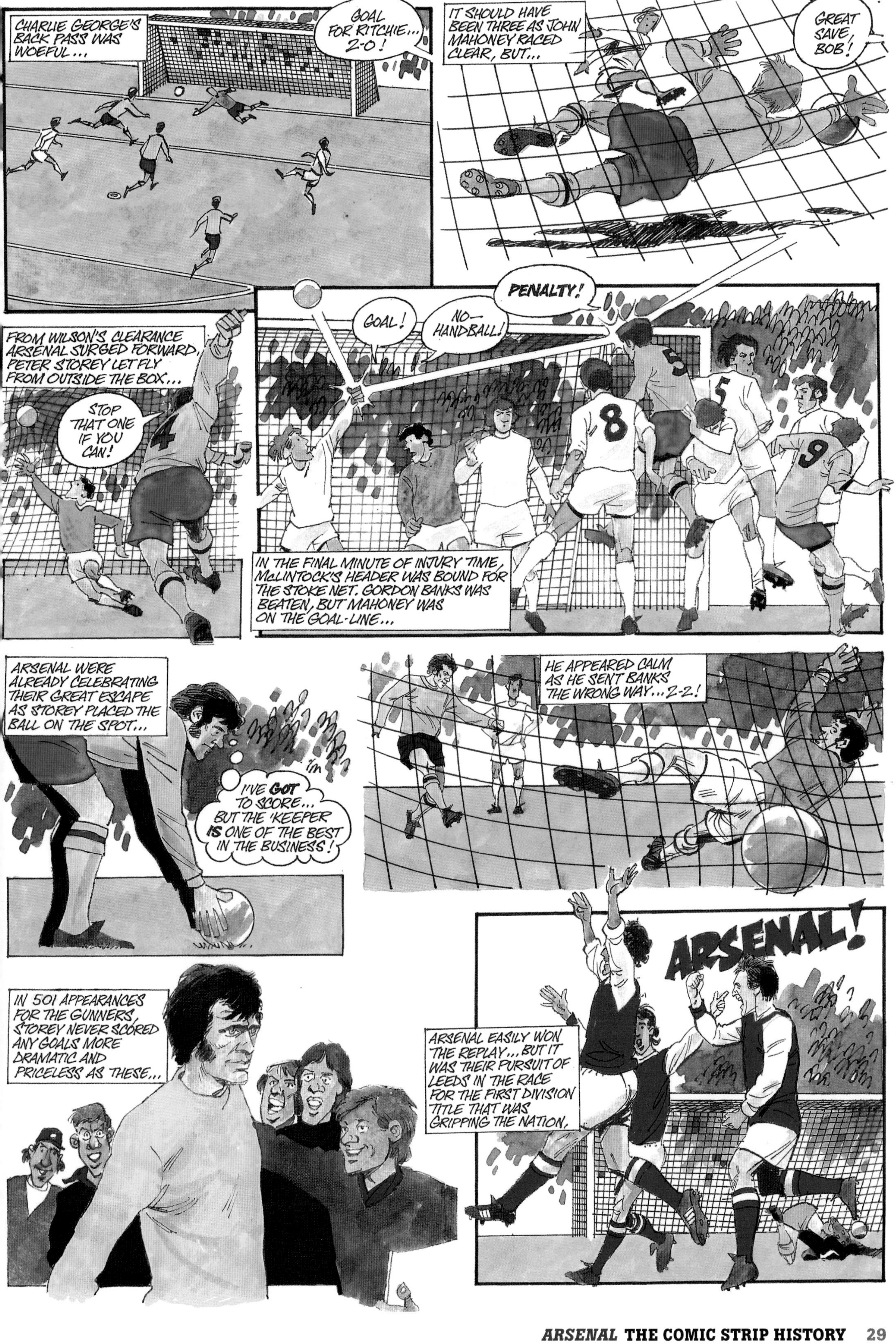

CHARLIE GEORGE'S BACK PASS WAS WOEFUL...
GOAL FOR RITCHIE... 2-0!
IT SHOULD HAVE BEEN THREE AS JOHN MAHONEY RACED CLEAR, BUT...
GREAT SAVE, BOB!
FROM WILSON'S CLEARANCE ARSENAL SURGED FORWARD, PETER STOREY LET FLY FROM OUTSIDE THE BOX...
STOP THAT ONE IF YOU CAN!
GOAL!
NO-HANDBALL!
PENALTY!
IN THE FINAL MINUTE OF INJURY TIME, McLINTOCK'S HEADER WAS BOUND FOR THE STOKE NET. GORDON BANKS WAS BEATEN, BUT MAHONEY WAS ON THE GOAL-LINE...
ARSENAL WERE ALREADY CELEBRATING THEIR GREAT ESCAPE AS STOREY PLACED THE BALL ON THE SPOT...
I'VE GOT TO SCORE... BUT THE 'KEEPER IS ONE OF THE BEST IN THE BUSINESS!
HE APPEARED CALM AS HE SENT BANKS THE WRONG WAY... 2-2!
IN 501 APPEARANCES FOR THE GUNNERS, STOREY NEVER SCORED ANY GOALS MORE DRAMATIC AND PRICELESS AS THESE...
ARSENAL!
ARSENAL EASILY WON THE REPLAY... BUT IT WAS THEIR PURSUIT OF LEEDS IN THE RACE FOR THE FIRST DIVISION TITLE THAT WAS GRIPPING THE NATION.

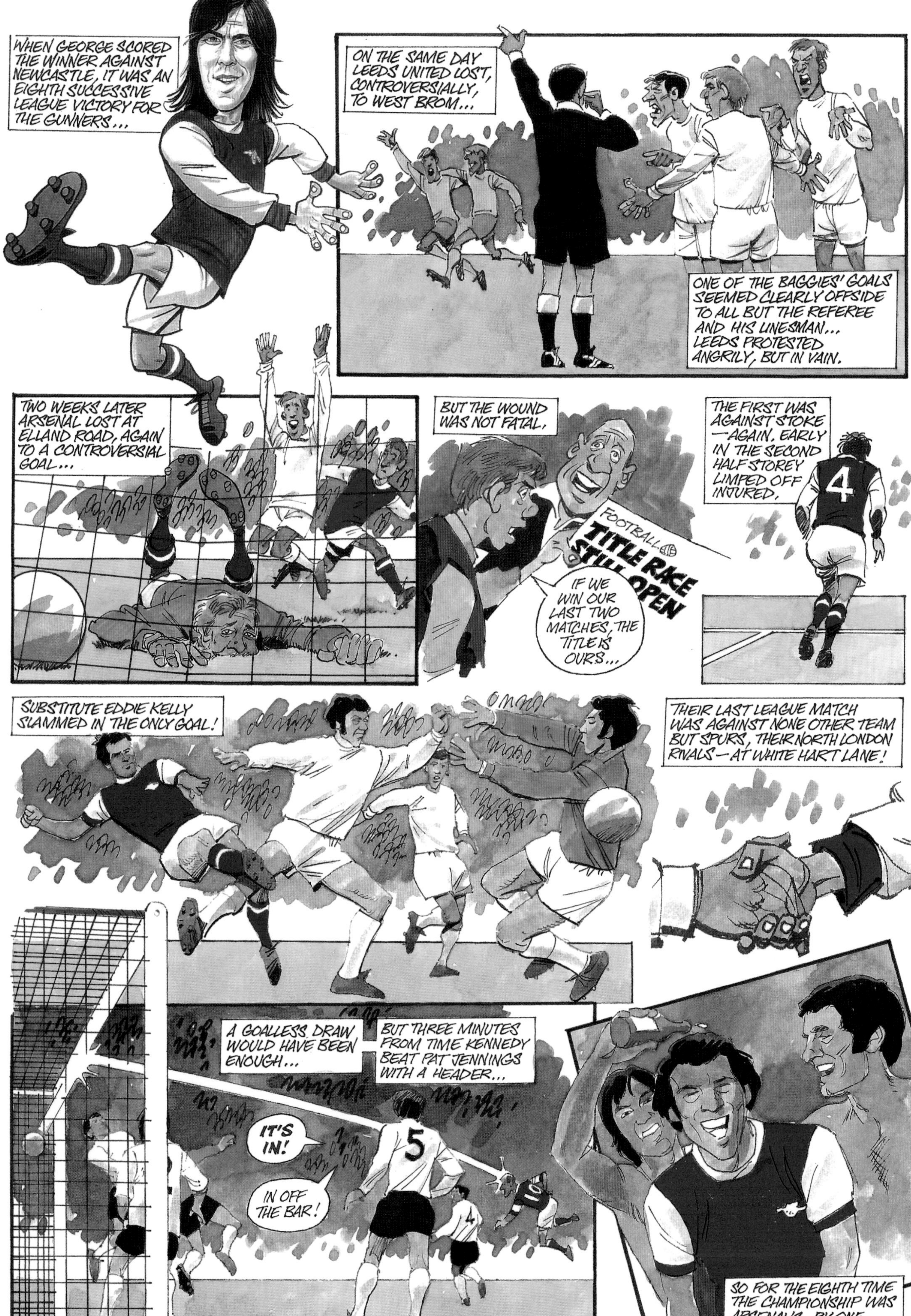

WHEN GEORGE SCORED THE WINNER AGAINST NEWCASTLE, IT WAS AN EIGHTH SUCCESSIVE LEAGUE VICTORY FOR THE GUNNERS...
ON THE SAME DAY LEEDS UNITED LOST, CONTROVERSIALLY, TO WEST BROM...
ONE OF THE BAGGIES' GOALS SEEMED CLEARLY OFFSIDE TO ALL BUT THE REFEREE AND HIS LINESMAN... LEEDS PROTESTED ANGRILY, BUT IN VAIN.
TWO WEEKS LATER ARSENAL LOST AT ELLAND ROAD, AGAIN TO A CONTROVERSIAL GOAL...
BUT THE WOUND WAS NOT FATAL.
FOOTBALL
TITLE RACE STILL OPEN
IF WE WIN OUR LAST TWO MATCHES, THE TITLE IS OURS...
THE FIRST WAS AGAINST STOKE —AGAIN. EARLY IN THE SECOND HALF STOREY LIMPED OFF INJURED.
SUBSTITUTE EDDIE KELLY SLAMMED IN THE ONLY GOAL!
THEIR LAST LEAGUE MATCH WAS AGAINST NONE OTHER TEAM BUT SPURS, THEIR NORTH LONDON RIVALS — AT WHITE HART LANE!
A GOALLESS DRAW WOULD HAVE BEEN ENOUGH...
BUT THREE MINUTES FROM TIME KENNEDY BEAT PAT JENNINGS WITH A HEADER...
IT'S IN!
IN OFF THE BAR!
SO FOR THE EIGHTH TIME THE CHAMPIONSHIP WAS ARSENAL'S, BY ONE POINT FROM LEEDS...

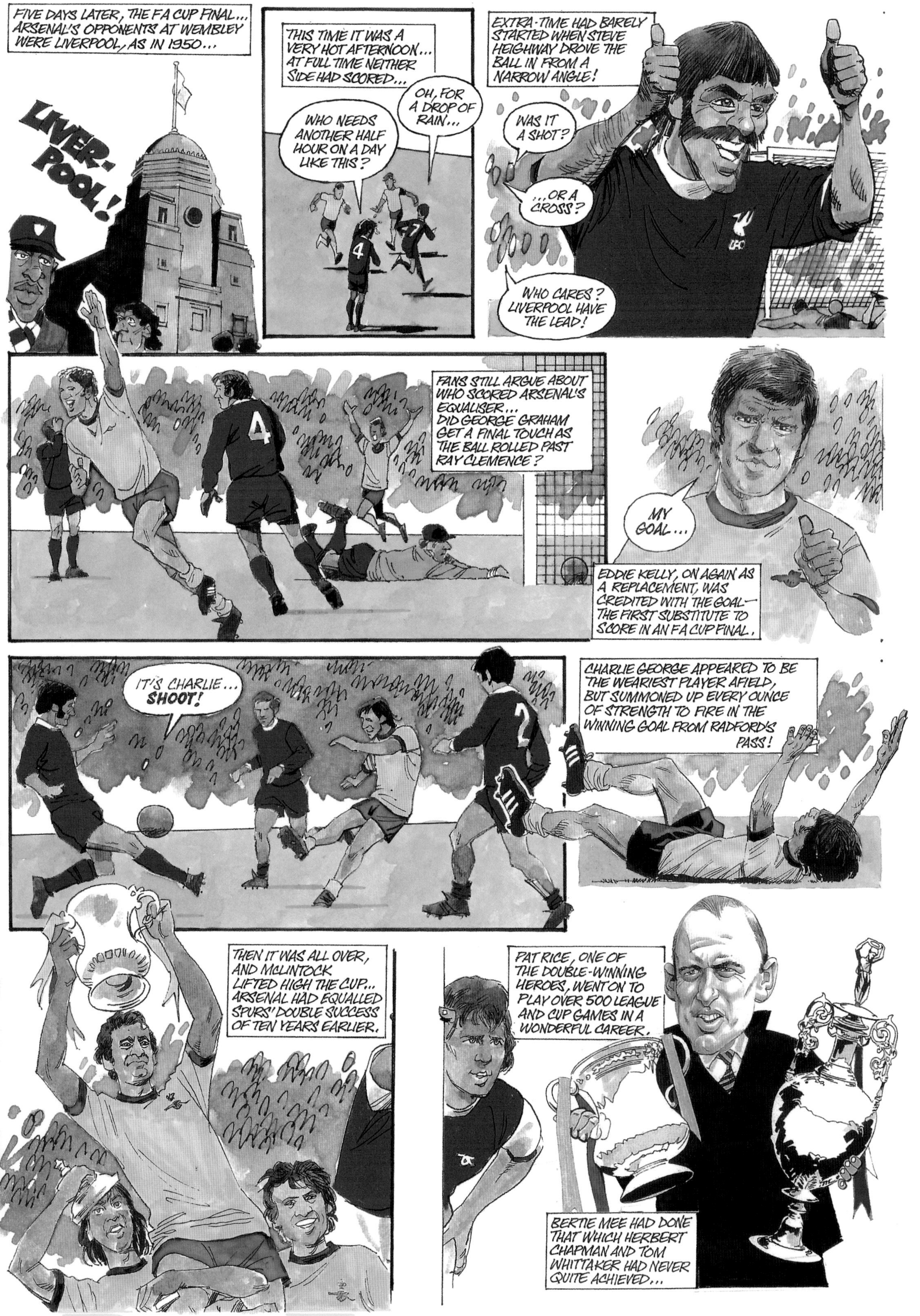
FIVE DAYS LATER, THE FA CUP FINAL... ARSENAL'S OPPONENTS AT WEMBLEY WERE LIVERPOOL, AS IN 1950...
LIVER-POOL!
THIS TIME IT WAS A VERY HOT AFTERNOON... AT FULL TIME NEITHER SIDE HAD SCORED...
WHO NEEDS ANOTHER HALF HOUR ON A DAY LIKE THIS?
OH, FOR A DROP OF RAIN...
EXTRA-TIME HAD BARELY STARTED WHEN STEVE HEIGHWAY DROVE THE BALL IN FROM A NARROW ANGLE!
WAS IT A SHOT?
...OR A CROSS?
WHO CARES? LIVERPOOL HAVE THE LEAD!
FANS STILL ARGUE ABOUT WHO SCORED ARSENAL'S EQUALISER... DID GEORGE GRAHAM GET A FINAL TOUCH AS THE BALL ROLLED PAST RAY CLEMENCE?
MY GOAL...
EDDIE KELLY, ON AGAIN AS A REPLACEMENT, WAS CREDITED WITH THE GOAL— THE FIRST SUBSTITUTE TO SCORE IN AN FA CUP FINAL.
IT'S CHARLIE... SHOOT!
CHARLIE GEORGE APPEARED TO BE THE WEARIEST PLAYER AFIELD, BUT SUMMONED UP EVERY OUNCE OF STRENGTH TO FIRE IN THE WINNING GOAL FROM RADFORD'S PASS!
THEN IT WAS ALL OVER, AND MCLINTOCK LIFTED HIGH THE CUP... ARSENAL HAD EQUALLED SPURS' DOUBLE SUCCESS OF TEN YEARS EARLIER.
PAT RICE, ONE OF THE DOUBLE-WINNING HEROES, WENT ON TO PLAY OVER 500 LEAGUE AND CUP GAMES IN A WONDERFUL CAREER.
BERTIE MEE HAD DONE THAT WHICH HERBERT CHAPMAN AND TOM WHITTAKER HAD NEVER QUITE ACHIEVED...

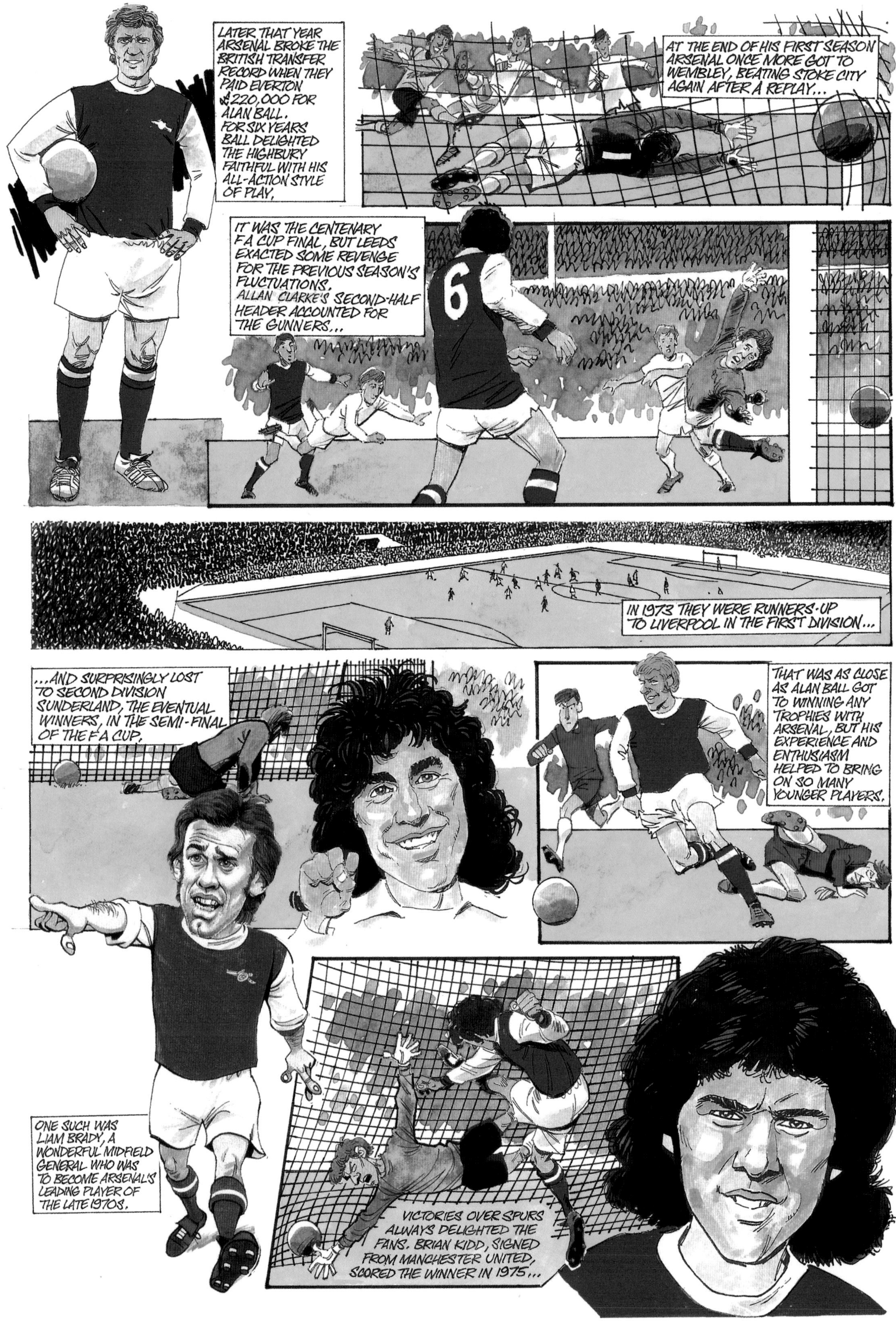
LATER THAT YEAR ARSENAL BROKE THE BRITISH TRANSFER RECORD WHEN THEY PAID EVERTON £220,000 FOR ALAN BALL. FOR SIX YEARS BALL DELIGHTED THE HIGHBURY FAITHFUL WITH HIS ALL-ACTION STYLE OF PLAY.
AT THE END OF HIS FIRST SEASON ARSENAL ONCE MORE GOT TO WEMBLEY, BEATING STOKE CITY AGAIN AFTER A REPLAY...
IT WAS THE CENTENARY F A CUP FINAL, BUT LEEDS EXACTED SOME REVENGE FOR THE PREVIOUS SEASON'S FLUCTUATIONS. ALLAN CLARKE'S SECOND-HALF HEADER ACCOUNTED FOR THE GUNNERS...
6
IN 1973 THEY WERE RUNNERS-UP TO LIVERPOOL IN THE FIRST DIVISION...
...AND SURPRISINGLY LOST TO SECOND DIVISION SUNDERLAND, THE EVENTUAL WINNERS, IN THE SEMI-FINAL OF THE F A CUP.
THAT WAS AS CLOSE AS ALAN BALL GOT TO WINNING ANY TROPHIES WITH ARSENAL, BUT HIS EXPERIENCE AND ENTHUSIASM HELPED TO BRING ON SO MANY YOUNGER PLAYERS.
ONE SUCH WAS LIAM BRADY, A WONDERFUL MIDFIELD GENERAL WHO WAS TO BECOME ARSENAL'S LEADING PLAYER OF THE LATE 1970S.
VICTORIES OVER SPURS ALWAYS DELIGHTED THE FANS. BRIAN KIDD, SIGNED FROM MANCHESTER UNITED, SCORED THE WINNER IN 1975...

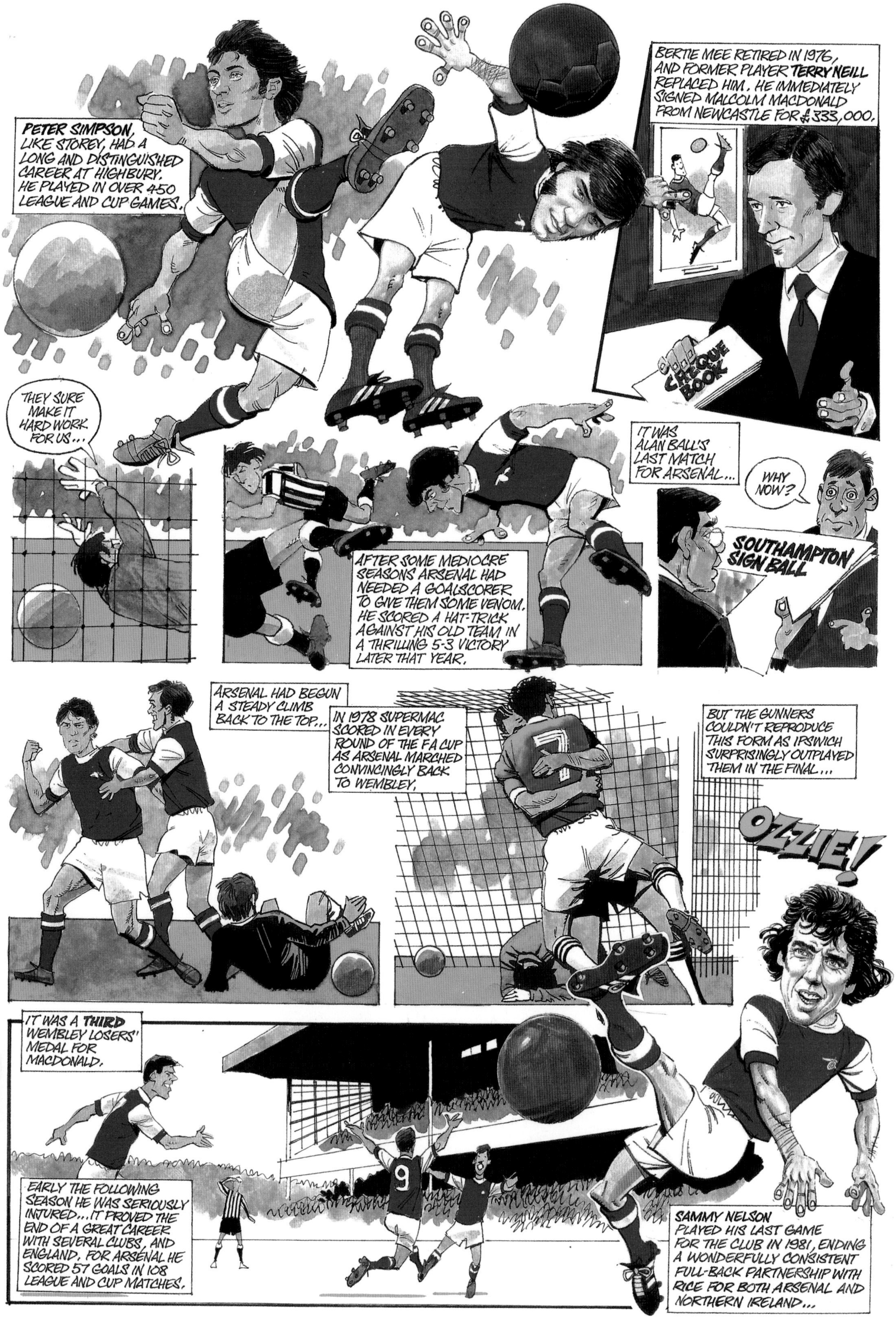
PETER SIMPSON, LIKE STOREY, HAD A LONG AND DISTINGUISHED CAREER AT HIGHBURY. HE PLAYED IN OVER 450 LEAGUE AND CUP GAMES.
BERTIE MEE RETIRED IN 1976, AND FORMER PLAYER TERRY NEILL REPLACED HIM. HE IMMEDIATELY SIGNED MALCOLM MACDONALD FROM NEWCASTLE FOR £333,000.
CHEQUE BOOK
THEY SURE MAKE IT HARD WORK FOR US...
AFTER SOME MEDIOCRE SEASONS ARSENAL HAD NEEDED A GOALSCORER TO GIVE THEM SOME VENOM. HE SCORED A HAT-TRICK AGAINST HIS OLD TEAM IN A THRILLING 5-3 VICTORY LATER THAT YEAR.
IT WAS ALAN BALL'S LAST MATCH FOR ARSENAL...
WHY NOW?
SOUTHAMPTON SIGN BALL
ARSENAL HAD BEGUN A STEADY CLIMB BACK TO THE TOP...
IN 1978 SUPERMAC SCORED IN EVERY ROUND OF THE FA CUP AS ARSENAL MARCHED CONVINCINGLY BACK TO WEMBLEY.
BUT THE GUNNERS COULDN'T REPRODUCE THIS FORM AS IPSWICH SURPRISINGLY OUTPLAYED THEM IN THE FINAL...
OZZIE!
IT WAS A THIRD WEMBLEY LOSERS' MEDAL FOR MACDONALD.
EARLY THE FOLLOWING SEASON HE WAS SERIOUSLY INJURED... IT PROVED THE END OF A GREAT CAREER WITH SEVERAL CLUBS, AND ENGLAND. FOR ARSENAL HE SCORED 57 GOALS IN 108 LEAGUE AND CUP MATCHES.
SAMMY NELSON PLAYED HIS LAST GAME FOR THE CLUB IN 1981, ENDING A WONDERFULLY CONSISTENT FULL-BACK PARTNERSHIP WITH RICE FOR BOTH ARSENAL AND NORTHERN IRELAND...

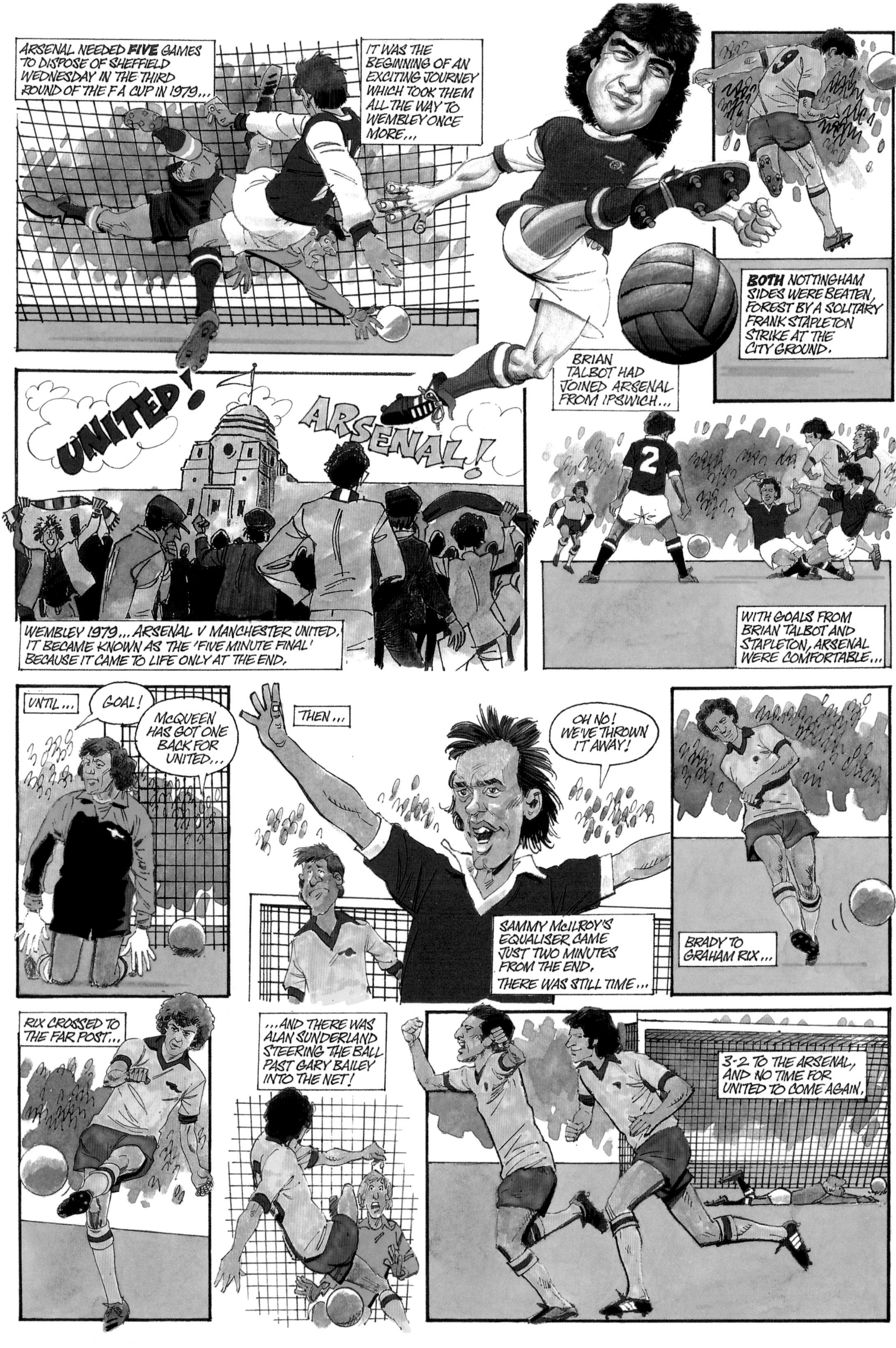
ARSENAL NEEDED FIVE GAMES TO DISPOSE OF SHEFFIELD WEDNESDAY IN THE THIRD ROUND OF THE F A CUP IN 1979...
IT WAS THE BEGINNING OF AN EXCITING JOURNEY WHICH TOOK THEM ALL THE WAY TO WEMBLEY ONCE MORE...
BOTH NOTTINGHAM SIDES WERE BEATEN, FOREST BY A SOLITARY FRANK STAPLETON STRIKE AT THE CITY GROUND.
UNITED!
ARSENAL!
WEMBLEY 1979... ARSENAL V MANCHESTER UNITED. IT BECAME KNOWN AS THE 'FIVE MINUTE FINAL' BECAUSE IT CAME TO LIFE ONLY AT THE END.
BRIAN TALBOT HAD JOINED ARSENAL FROM IPSWICH...
2
WITH GOALS FROM BRIAN TALBOT AND STAPLETON, ARSENAL WERE COMFORTABLE...
UNTIL...
GOAL!
McQUEEN HAS GOT ONE BACK FOR UNITED...
THEN...
OH NO! WE'VE THROWN IT AWAY!
SAMMY McILROY'S EQUALISER CAME JUST TWO MINUTES FROM THE END.
THERE WAS STILL TIME...
BRADY TO GRAHAM RIX...
RIX CROSSED TO THE FAR POST...
...AND THERE WAS ALAN SUNDERLAND STEERING THE BALL PAST GARY BAILEY INTO THE NET!
3-2 TO THE ARSENAL, AND NO TIME FOR UNITED TO COME AGAIN.

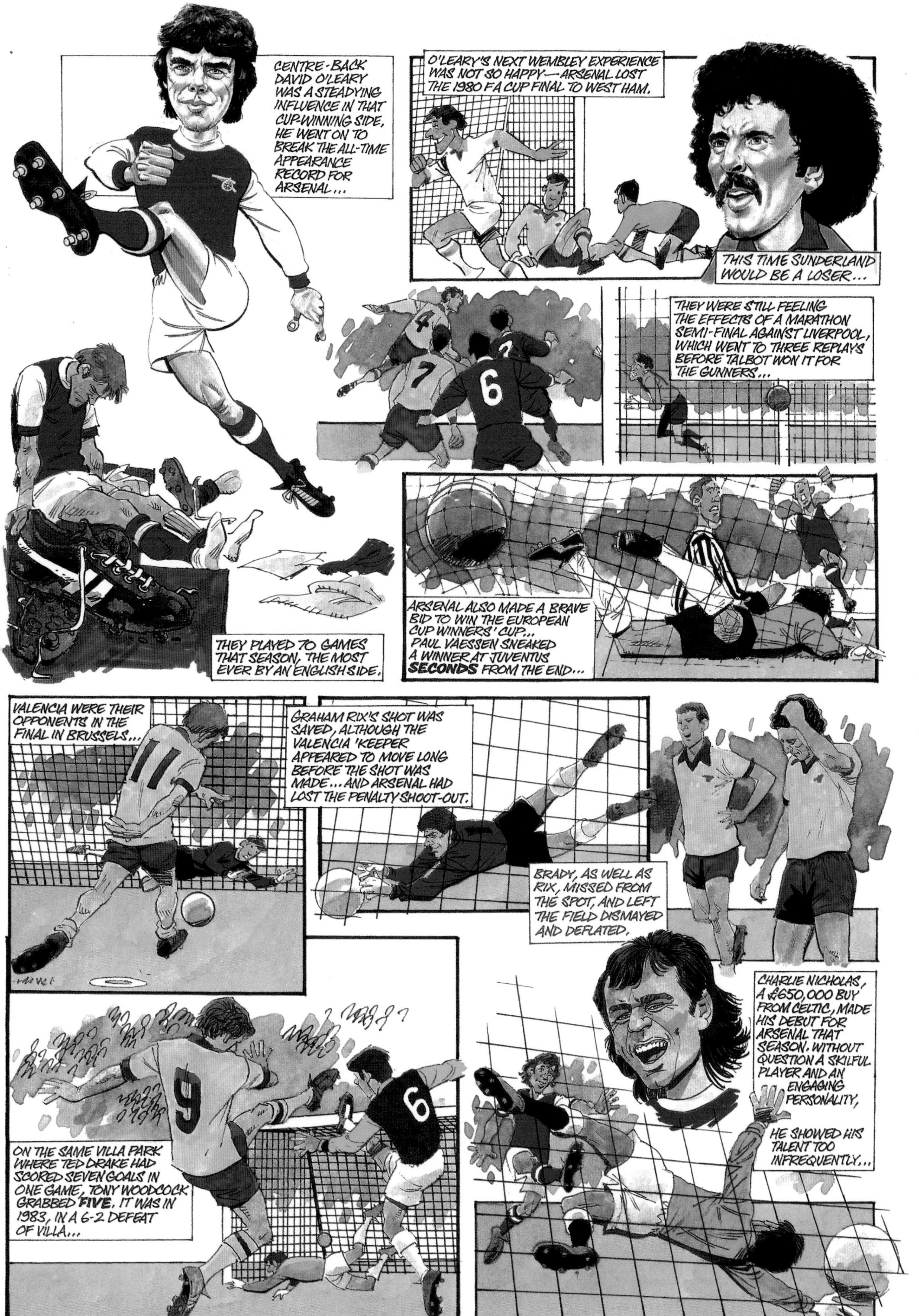
CENTRE-BACK DAVID O'LEARY WAS A STEADYING INFLUENCE IN THAT CUP-WINNING SIDE. HE WENT ON TO BREAK THE ALL-TIME APPEARANCE RECORD FOR ARSENAL...
O'LEARY'S NEXT WEMBLEY EXPERIENCE WAS NOT SO HAPPY — ARSENAL LOST THE 1980 FA CUP FINAL TO WEST HAM.
THIS TIME SUNDERLAND WOULD BE A LOSER...
THEY WERE STILL FEELING THE EFFECTS OF A MARATHON SEMI-FINAL AGAINST LIVERPOOL, WHICH WENT TO THREE REPLAYS BEFORE TALBOT WON IT FOR THE GUNNERS...
THEY PLAYED 70 GAMES THAT SEASON, THE MOST EVER BY AN ENGLISH SIDE.
ARSENAL ALSO MADE A BRAVE BID TO WIN THE EUROPEAN CUP WINNERS' CUP... PAUL VAESSEN SNEAKED A WINNER AT JUVENTUS SECONDS FROM THE END...
VALENCIA WERE THEIR OPPONENTS IN THE FINAL IN BRUSSELS...
GRAHAM RIX'S SHOT WAS SAVED, ALTHOUGH THE VALENCIA 'KEEPER APPEARED TO MOVE LONG BEFORE THE SHOT WAS MADE... AND ARSENAL HAD LOST THE PENALTY SHOOT-OUT.
BRADY, AS WELL AS RIX, MISSED FROM THE SPOT, AND LEFT THE FIELD DISMAYED AND DEFLATED.
ON THE SAME VILLA PARK WHERE TED DRAKE HAD SCORED SEVEN GOALS IN ONE GAME, TONY WOODCOCK GRABBED FIVE. IT WAS IN 1983, IN A 6-2 DEFEAT OF VILLA...
CHARLIE NICHOLAS, A £650,000 BUY FROM CELTIC, MADE HIS DEBUT FOR ARSENAL THAT SEASON. WITHOUT QUESTION A SKILFUL PLAYER AND AN ENGAGING PERSONALITY,
HE SHOWED HIS TALENT TOO INFREQUENTLY...

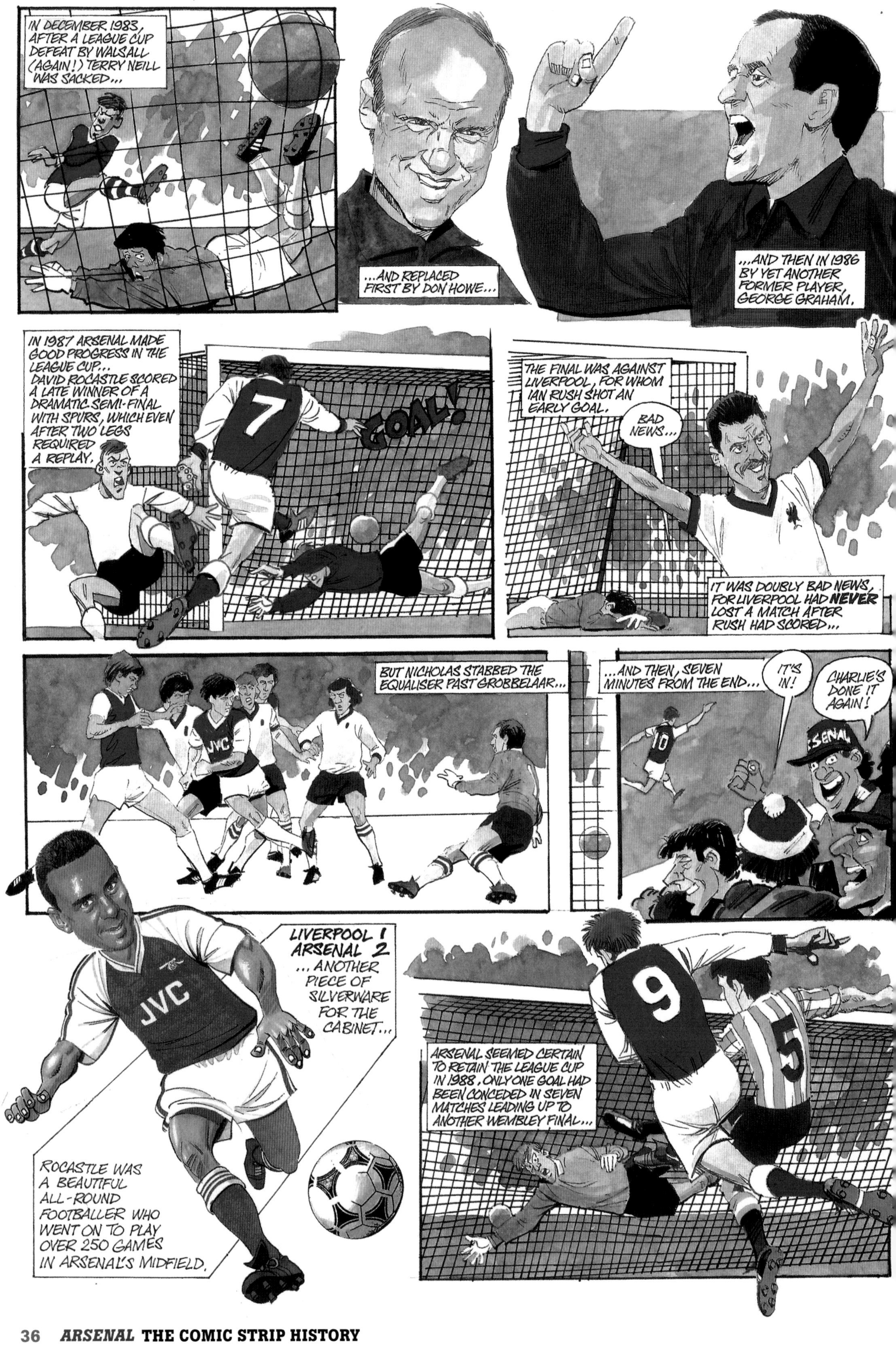
IN DECEMBER 1983, AFTER A LEAGUE CUP DEFEAT BY WALSALL (AGAIN!) TERRY NEILL WAS SACKED...
...AND REPLACED FIRST BY DON HOWE...
...AND THEN IN 1986 BY YET ANOTHER FORMER PLAYER, GEORGE GRAHAM.
IN 1987 ARSENAL MADE GOOD PROGRESS IN THE LEAGUE CUP... DAVID ROCASTLE SCORED A LATE WINNER OF A DRAMATIC SEMI-FINAL WITH SPURS, WHICH EVEN AFTER TWO LEGS REQUIRED A REPLAY.
GOAL!
THE FINAL WAS AGAINST LIVERPOOL, FOR WHOM IAN RUSH SHOT AN EARLY GOAL.
BAD NEWS...
IT WAS DOUBLY BAD NEWS, FOR LIVERPOOL HAD NEVER LOST A MATCH AFTER RUSH HAD SCORED...
BUT NICHOLAS STABBED THE EQUALISER PAST GROBBELAAR...
...AND THEN, SEVEN MINUTES FROM THE END...
IT'S IN!
CHARLIE'S DONE IT AGAIN!
LIVERPOOL 1 ARSENAL 2 ...ANOTHER PIECE OF SILVERWARE FOR THE CABINET...
ARSENAL SEEMED CERTAIN TO RETAIN THE LEAGUE CUP IN 1988, ONLY ONE GOAL HAD BEEN CONCEDED IN SEVEN MATCHES LEADING UP TO ANOTHER WEMBLEY FINAL...
ROCASTLE WAS A BEAUTIFUL ALL-ROUND FOOTBALLER WHO WENT ON TO PLAY OVER 250 GAMES IN ARSENAL'S MIDFIELD.

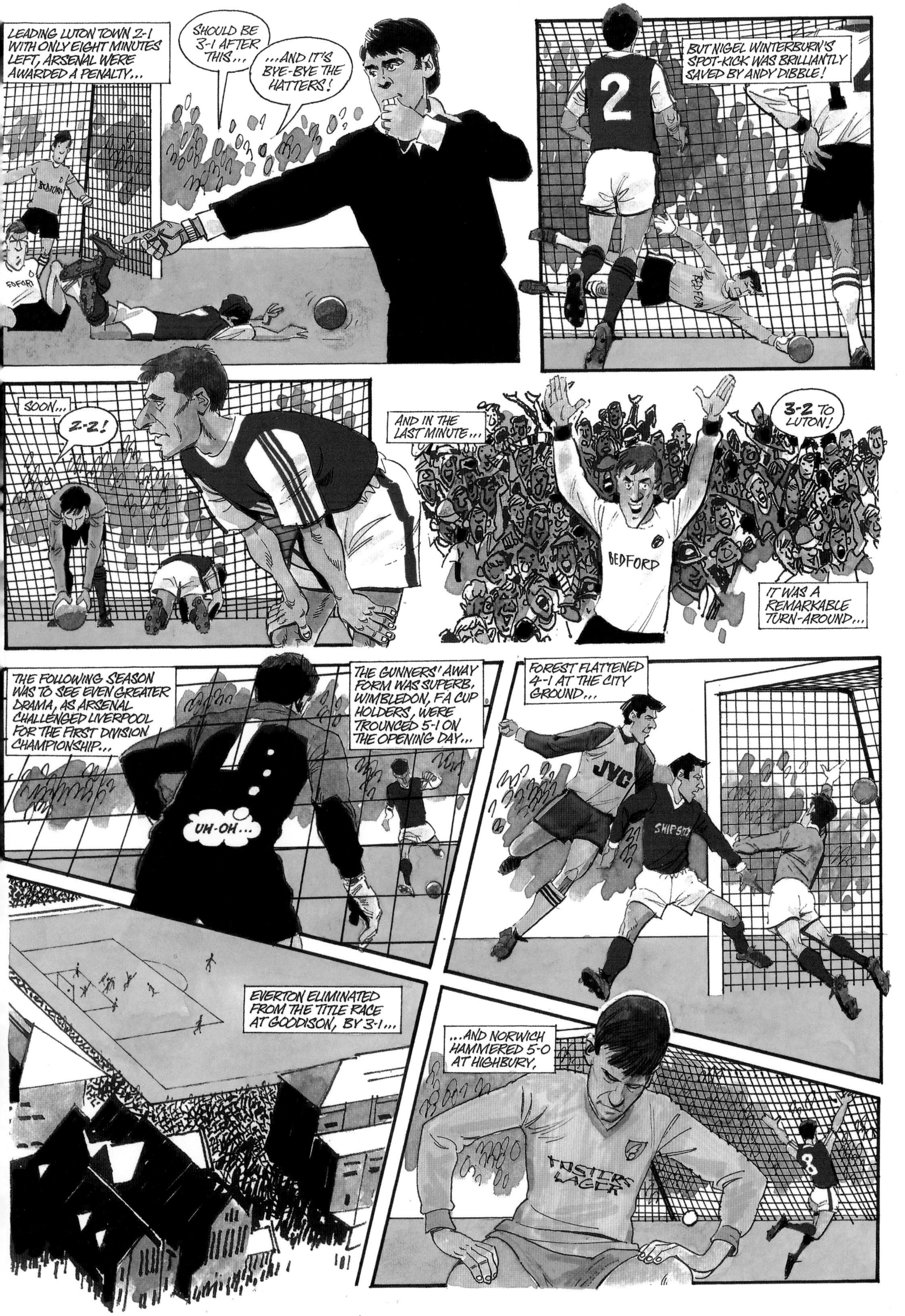
LEADING LUTON TOWN 2-1 WITH ONLY EIGHT MINUTES LEFT, ARSENAL WERE AWARDED A PENALTY...
SHOULD BE 3-1 AFTER THIS...
...AND IT'S BYE-BYE THE HATTERS!
BUT NIGEL WINTERBURN'S SPOT-KICK WAS BRILLIANTLY SAVED BY ANDY DIBBLE!
SOON...
2-2!
AND IN THE LAST MINUTE...
3-2 TO LUTON!
BEDFORD
IT WAS A REMARKABLE TURN-AROUND...
THE FOLLOWING SEASON WAS TO SEE EVEN GREATER DRAMA, AS ARSENAL CHALLENGED LIVERPOOL FOR THE FIRST DIVISION CHAMPIONSHIP...
THE GUNNERS' AWAY FORM WAS SUPERB, WIMBLEDON, FA CUP HOLDERS, WERE TROUNCED 5-1 ON THE OPENING DAY...
UH-OH...
FOREST FLATTENED 4-1 AT THE CITY GROUND...
JVC
EVERTON ELIMINATED FROM THE TITLE RACE AT GOODISON, BY 3-1...
...AND NORWICH HAMMERED 5-0 AT HIGHBURY.
FOSTERS LAGER

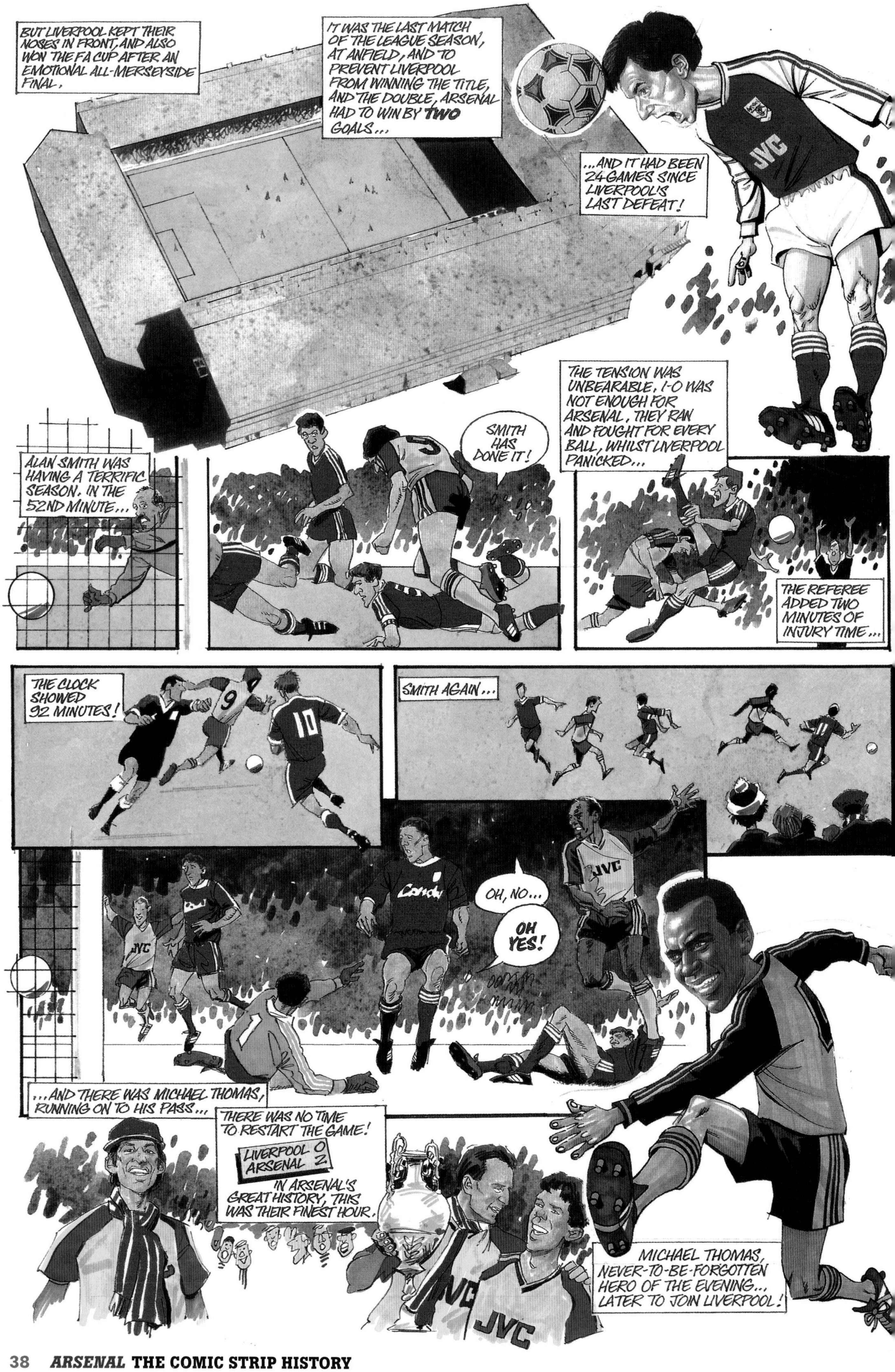
BUT LIVERPOOL KEPT THEIR NOSES IN FRONT, AND ALSO WON THE FA CUP AFTER AN EMOTIONAL ALL-MERSEYSIDE FINAL.
IT WAS THE LAST MATCH OF THE LEAGUE SEASON, AT ANFIELD, AND TO PREVENT LIVERPOOL FROM WINNING THE TITLE, AND THE DOUBLE, ARSENAL HAD TO WIN BY TWO GOALS...
...AND IT HAD BEEN 24 GAMES SINCE LIVERPOOL'S LAST DEFEAT!
JVC
THE TENSION WAS UNBEARABLE. 1-0 WAS NOT ENOUGH FOR ARSENAL, THEY RAN AND FOUGHT FOR EVERY BALL, WHILST LIVERPOOL PANICKED...
ALAN SMITH WAS HAVING A TERRIFIC SEASON. IN THE 52ND MINUTE...
SMITH HAS DONE IT!
THE REFEREE ADDED TWO MINUTES OF INJURY TIME...
THE CLOCK SHOWED 92 MINUTES!
SMITH AGAIN...
OH, NO...
OH YES!
...AND THERE WAS MICHAEL THOMAS, RUNNING ON TO HIS PASS...
THERE WAS NO TIME TO RESTART THE GAME!
LIVERPOOL 0
ARSENAL 2
IN ARSENAL'S GREAT HISTORY, THIS WAS THEIR FINEST HOUR.
MICHAEL THOMAS, NEVER-TO-BE-FORGOTTEN HERO OF THE EVENING... LATER TO JOIN LIVERPOOL!

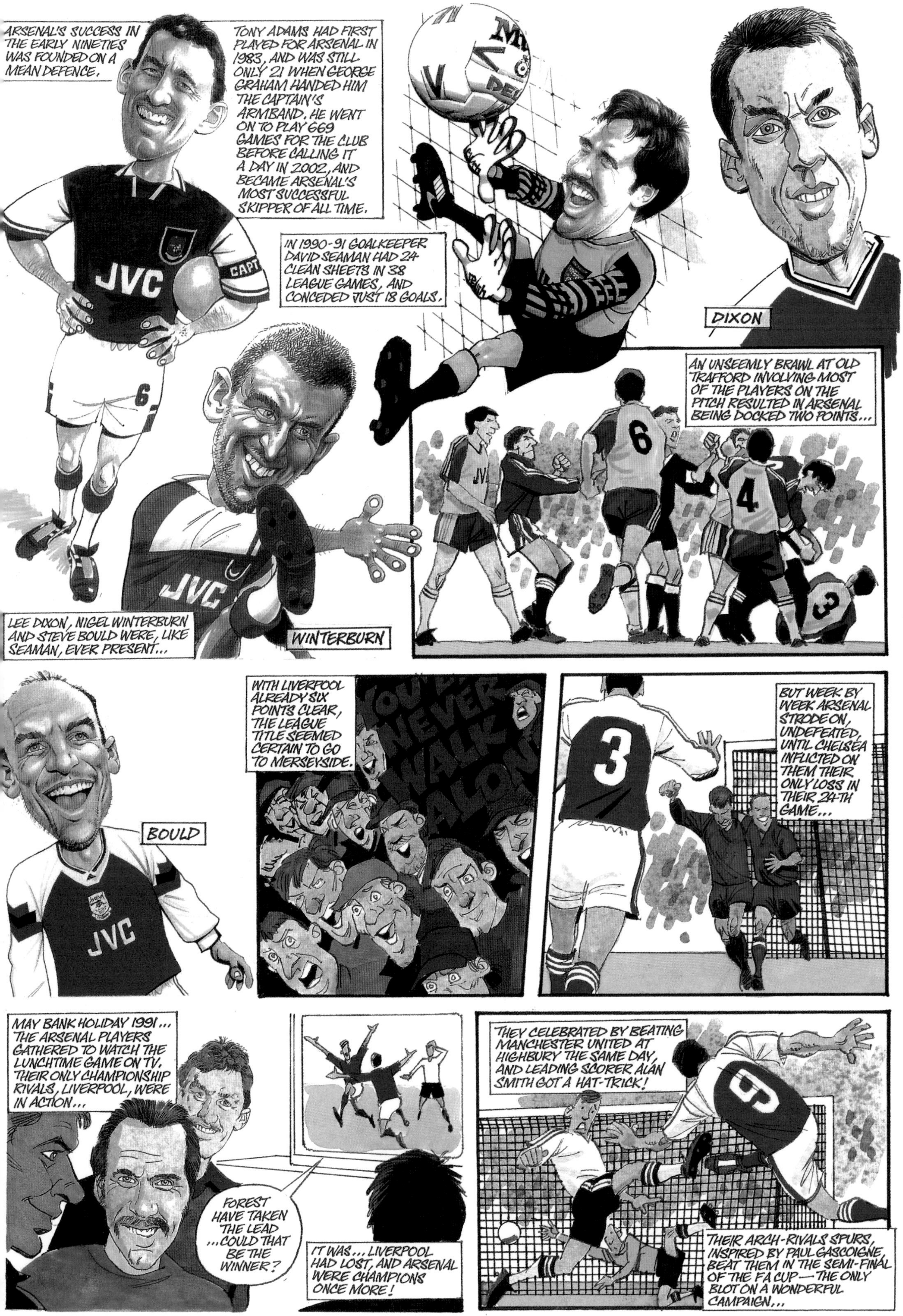
ARSENAL'S SUCCESS IN THE EARLY NINETIES WAS FOUNDED ON A MEAN DEFENCE.
TONY ADAMS HAD FIRST PLAYED FOR ARSENAL IN 1983, AND WAS STILL ONLY 21 WHEN GEORGE GRAHAM HANDED HIM THE CAPTAIN'S ARMBAND. HE WENT ON TO PLAY 669 GAMES FOR THE CLUB BEFORE CALLING IT A DAY IN 2002, AND BECAME ARSENAL'S MOST SUCCESSFUL SKIPPER OF ALL TIME.
JVC
CAPT
IN 1990-91 GOALKEEPER DAVID SEAMAN HAD 24 CLEAN SHEETS IN 38 LEAGUE GAMES, AND CONCEDED JUST 18 GOALS.
DIXON
AN UNSEEMLY BRAWL AT OLD TRAFFORD INVOLVING MOST OF THE PLAYERS ON THE PITCH RESULTED IN ARSENAL BEING DOCKED TWO POINTS...
JVC
LEE DIXON, NIGEL WINTERBURN AND STEVE BOULD WERE, LIKE SEAMAN, EVER PRESENT...
WINTERBURN
BOULD
JVC
WITH LIVERPOOL ALREADY SIX POINTS CLEAR, THE LEAGUE TITLE SEEMED CERTAIN TO GO TO MERSEYSIDE.
BUT WEEK BY WEEK ARSENAL STRODE ON, UNDEFEATED, UNTIL CHELSEA INFLICTED ON THEM THEIR ONLY LOSS IN THEIR 24TH GAME...
MAY BANK HOLIDAY 1991... THE ARSENAL PLAYERS GATHERED TO WATCH THE LUNCHTIME GAME ON TV. THEIR ONLY CHAMPIONSHIP RIVALS, LIVERPOOL, WERE IN ACTION...
FOREST HAVE TAKEN THE LEAD ...COULD THAT BE THE WINNER?
IT WAS... LIVERPOOL HAD LOST, AND ARSENAL WERE CHAMPIONS ONCE MORE!
THEY CELEBRATED BY BEATING MANCHESTER UNITED AT HIGHBURY THE SAME DAY, AND LEADING SCORER ALAN SMITH GOT A HAT-TRICK!
THEIR ARCH-RIVALS SPURS, INSPIRED BY PAUL GASCOIGNE, BEAT THEM IN THE SEMI-FINAL OF THE FA CUP — THE ONLY BLOT ON A WONDERFUL CAMPAIGN...

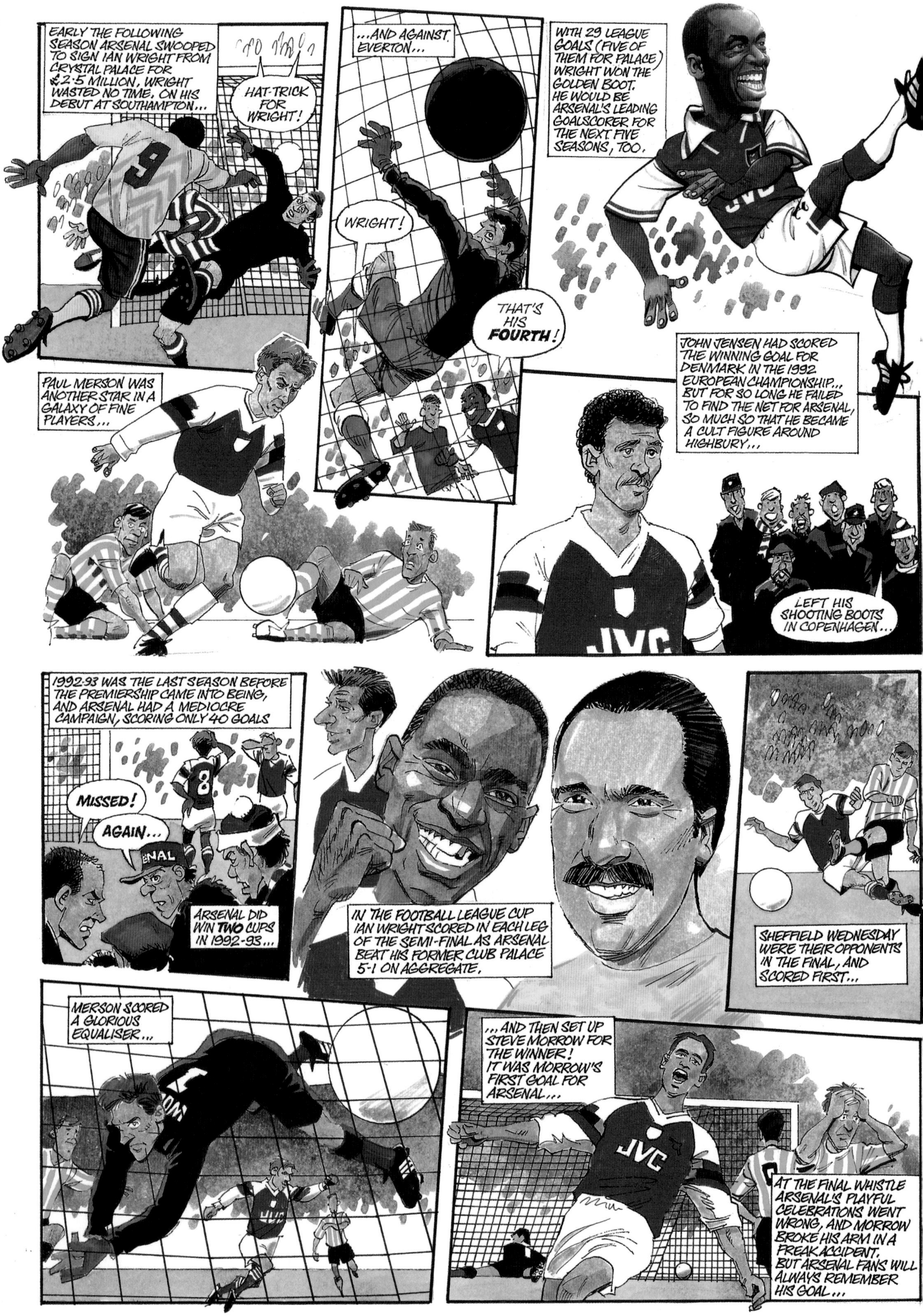
EARLY THE FOLLOWING SEASON ARSENAL SWOOPED TO SIGN IAN WRIGHT FROM CRYSTAL PALACE FOR £2·5 MILLION. WRIGHT WASTED NO TIME, ON HIS DEBUT AT SOUTHAMPTON...
HAT-TRICK FOR WRIGHT!
...AND AGAINST EVERTON...
WRIGHT!
THAT'S HIS **FOURTH**!
WITH 29 LEAGUE GOALS (FIVE OF THEM FOR PALACE) WRIGHT WON THE GOLDEN BOOT. HE WOULD BE ARSENAL'S LEADING GOALSCORER FOR THE NEXT FIVE SEASONS, TOO.
PAUL MERSON WAS ANOTHER STAR IN A GALAXY OF FINE PLAYERS...
JOHN JENSEN HAD SCORED THE WINNING GOAL FOR DENMARK IN THE 1992 EUROPEAN CHAMPIONSHIP... BUT FOR SO LONG HE FAILED TO FIND THE NET FOR ARSENAL, SO MUCH SO THAT HE BECAME A CULT FIGURE AROUND HIGHBURY...
LEFT HIS SHOOTING BOOTS IN COPENHAGEN...
1992-93 WAS THE LAST SEASON BEFORE THE PREMIERSHIP CAME INTO BEING, AND ARSENAL HAD A MEDIOCRE CAMPAIGN, SCORING ONLY 40 GOALS
MISSED!
AGAIN...
ARSENAL DID WIN **TWO** CUPS IN 1992-93...
IN THE FOOTBALL LEAGUE CUP IAN WRIGHT SCORED IN EACH LEG OF THE SEMI-FINAL AS ARSENAL BEAT HIS FORMER CLUB PALACE 5-1 ON AGGREGATE.
SHEFFIELD WEDNESDAY WERE THEIR OPPONENTS IN THE FINAL, AND SCORED FIRST...
MERSON SCORED A GLORIOUS EQUALISER...
...AND THEN SET UP STEVE MORROW FOR THE WINNER! IT WAS MORROW'S FIRST GOAL FOR ARSENAL...
AT THE FINAL WHISTLE ARSENAL'S PLAYFUL CELEBRATIONS WENT WRONG, AND MORROW BROKE HIS ARM IN A FREAK ACCIDENT, BUT ARSENAL FANS WILL ALWAYS REMEMBER HIS GOAL...

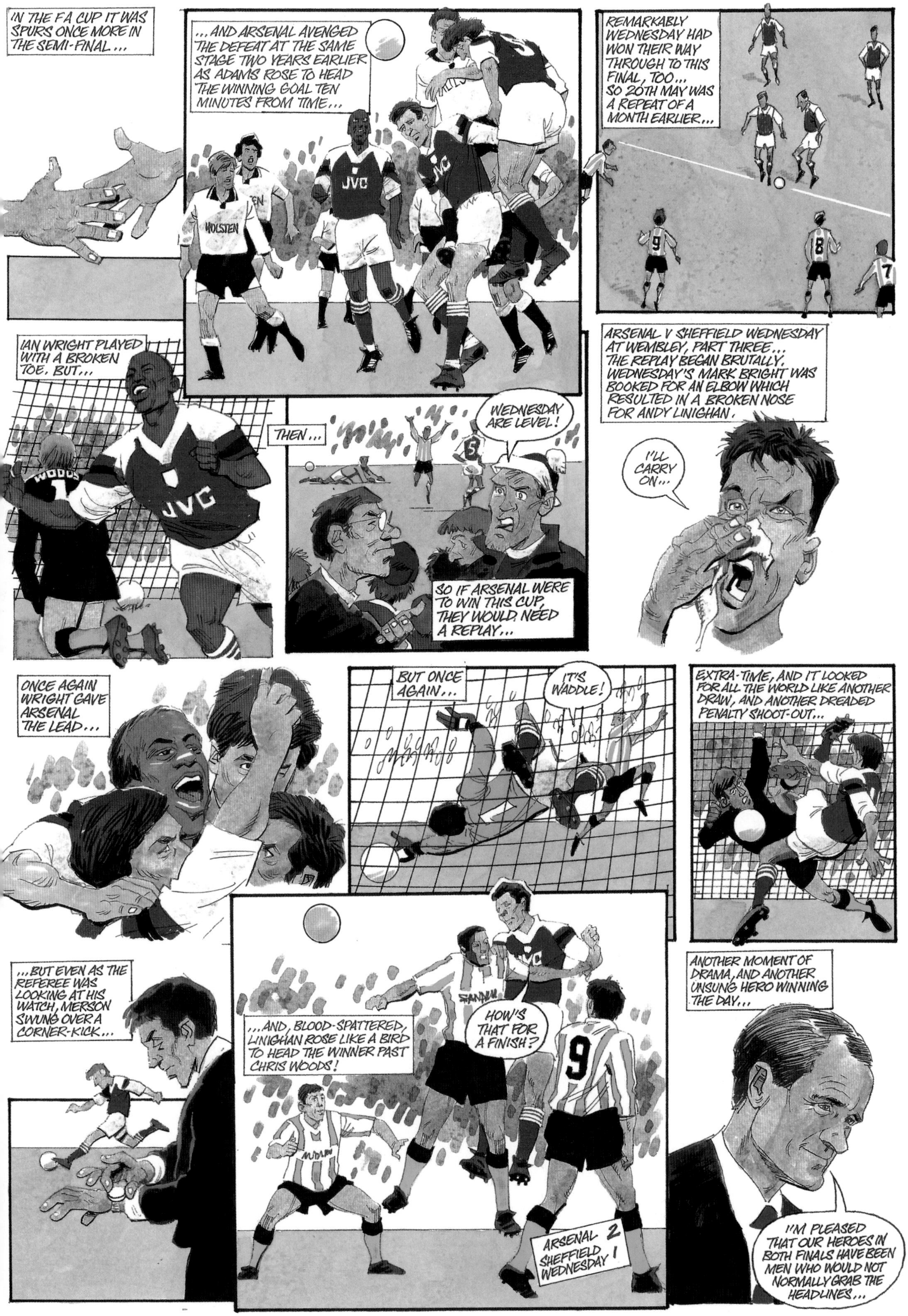
IN THE F.A CUP IT WAS SPURS ONCE MORE IN THE SEMI-FINAL...
...AND ARSENAL AVENGED THE DEFEAT AT THE SAME STAGE TWO YEARS EARLIER AS ADAMS ROSE TO HEAD THE WINNING GOAL TEN MINUTES FROM TIME...
REMARKABLY WEDNESDAY HAD WON THEIR WAY THROUGH TO THIS FINAL, TOO... SO 20TH MAY WAS A REPEAT OF A MONTH EARLIER...
IAN WRIGHT PLAYED WITH A BROKEN TOE. BUT...
THEN...
WEDNESDAY ARE LEVEL!
SO IF ARSENAL WERE TO WIN THIS CUP, THEY WOULD NEED A REPLAY...
ARSENAL V SHEFFIELD WEDNESDAY AT WEMBLEY, PART THREE... THE REPLAY BEGAN BRUTALLY. WEDNESDAY'S MARK BRIGHT WAS BOOKED FOR AN ELBOW WHICH RESULTED IN A BROKEN NOSE FOR ANDY LINIGHAN.
I'LL CARRY ON...
ONCE AGAIN WRIGHT GAVE ARSENAL THE LEAD...
BUT ONCE AGAIN...
IT'S WADDLE!
EXTRA-TIME, AND IT LOOKED FOR ALL THE WORLD LIKE ANOTHER DRAW, AND ANOTHER DREADED PENALTY SHOOT-OUT...
...BUT EVEN AS THE REFEREE WAS LOOKING AT HIS WATCH, MERSON SWUNG OVER A CORNER-KICK...
...AND, BLOOD-SPATTERED, LINIGHAN ROSE LIKE A BIRD TO HEAD THE WINNER PAST CHRIS WOODS!
HOW'S THAT FOR A FINISH?
ARSENAL 2
SHEFFIELD WEDNESDAY 1
ANOTHER MOMENT OF DRAMA, AND ANOTHER UNSUNG HERO WINNING THE DAY...
I'M PLEASED THAT OUR HEROES IN BOTH FINALS HAVE BEEN MEN WHO WOULD NOT NORMALLY GRAB THE HEADLINES...

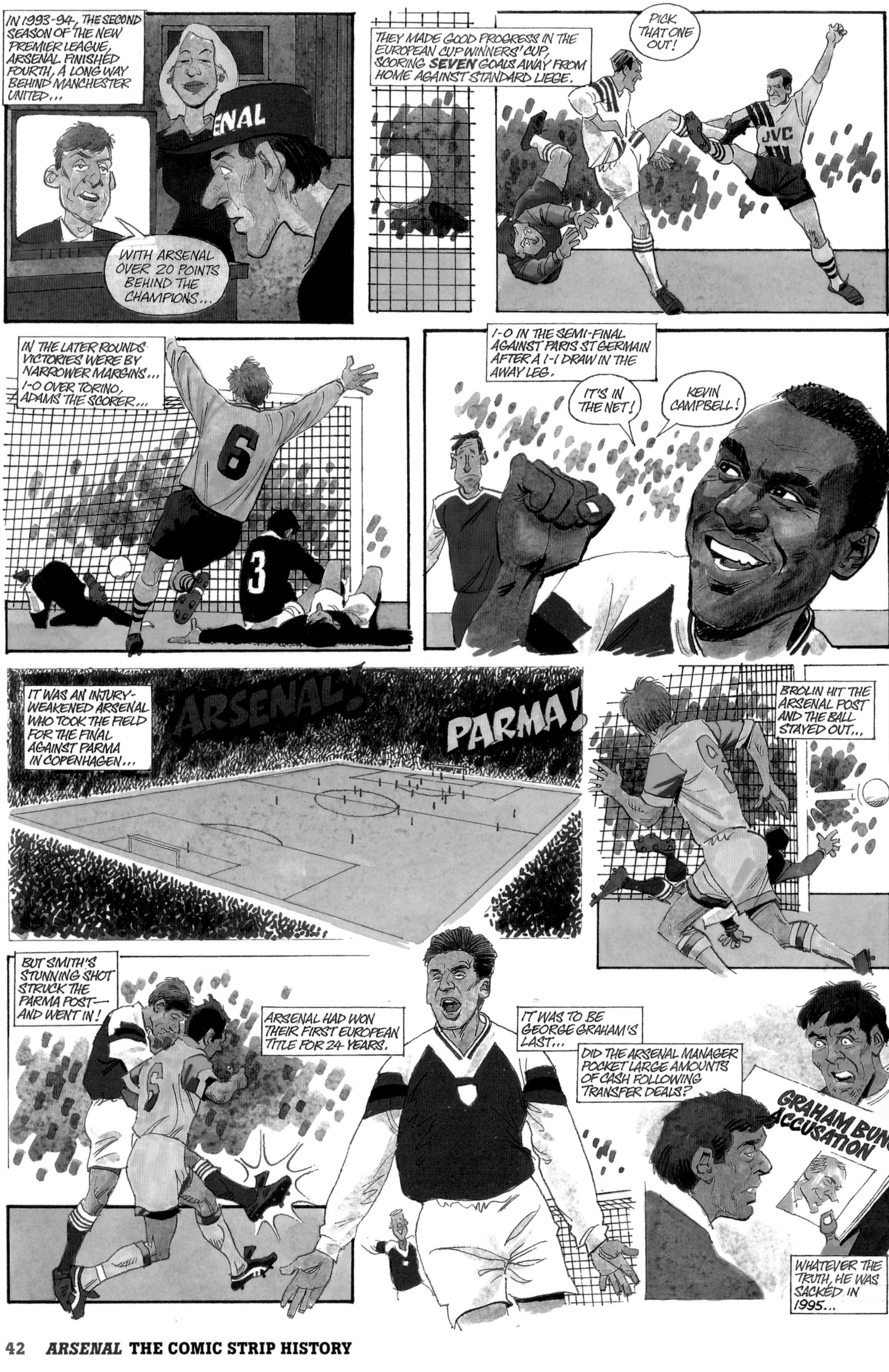
IN 1993-94, THE SECOND SEASON OF THE NEW PREMIER LEAGUE, ARSENAL FINISHED FOURTH, A LONG WAY BEHIND MANCHESTER UNITED...
ENAL
WITH ARSENAL OVER 20 POINTS BEHIND THE CHAMPIONS...
THEY MADE GOOD PROGRESS IN THE EUROPEAN CUP WINNERS' CUP, SCORING SEVEN GOALS AWAY FROM HOME AGAINST STANDARD LIEGE.
PICK THAT ONE OUT!
JVC
IN THE LATER ROUNDS VICTORIES WERE BY NARROWER MARGINS... 1-0 OVER TORINO, ADAMS THE SCORER...
1-0 IN THE SEMI-FINAL AGAINST PARIS ST GERMAIN AFTER A 1-1 DRAW IN THE AWAY LEG.
IT'S IN THE NET!
KEVIN CAMPBELL!
IT WAS AN INJURY-WEAKENED ARSENAL WHO TOOK THE FIELD FOR THE FINAL AGAINST PARMA IN COPENHAGEN...
ARSENAL!
PARMA!
BROLIN HIT THE ARSENAL POST AND THE BALL STAYED OUT...
BUT SMITH'S STUNNING SHOT STRUCK THE PARMA POST- AND WENT IN!
ARSENAL HAD WON THEIR FIRST EUROPEAN TITLE FOR 24 YEARS.
IT WAS TO BE GEORGE GRAHAM'S LAST...
DID THE ARSENAL MANAGER POCKET LARGE AMOUNTS OF CASH FOLLOWING TRANSFER DEALS?
GRAHAM BUNG ACCUSATION
WHATEVER THE TRUTH, HE WAS SACKED IN 1995...

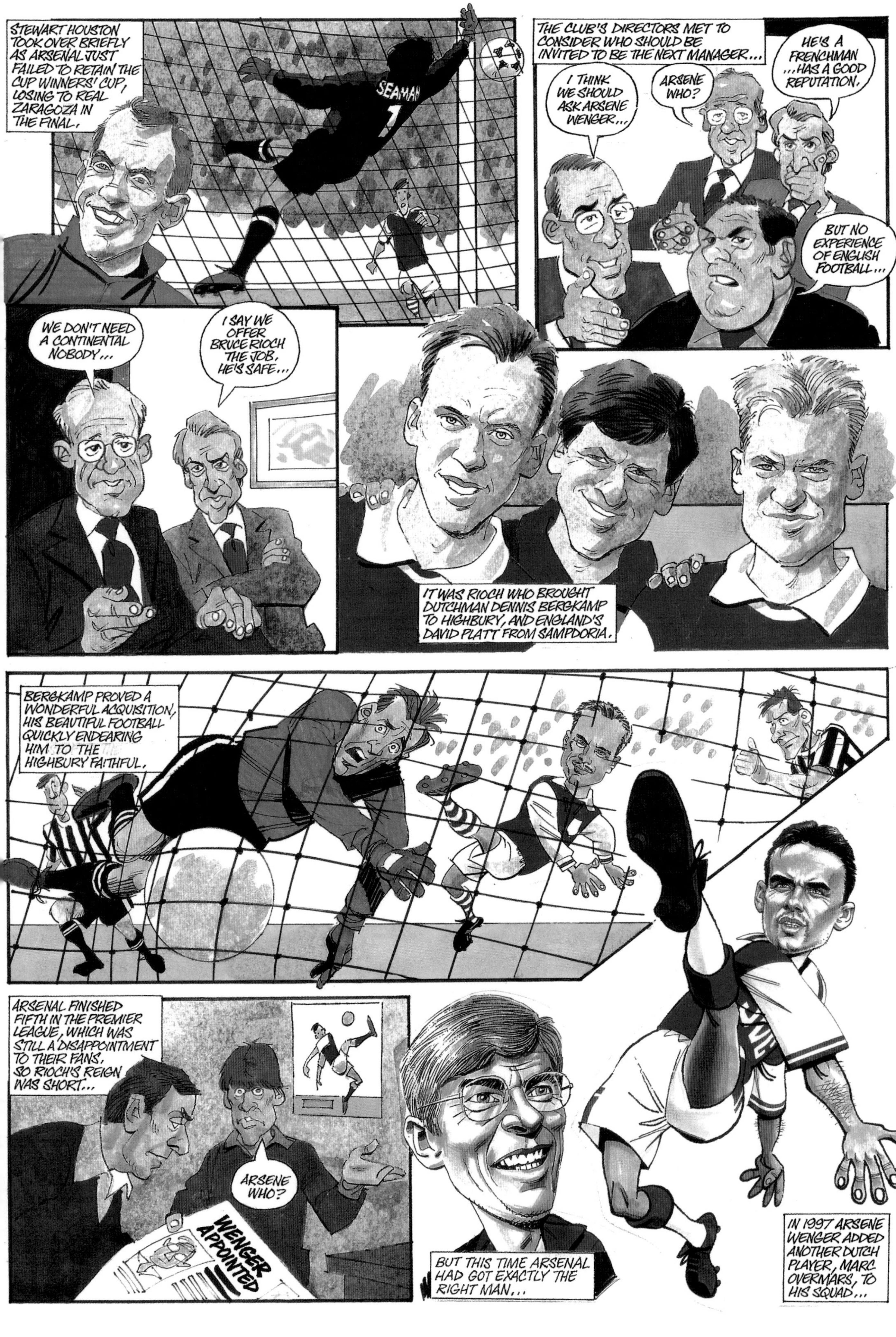

STEWART HOUSTON TOOK OVER BRIEFLY AS ARSENAL JUST FAILED TO RETAIN THE CUP WINNERS' CUP, LOSING TO REAL ZARAGOZA IN THE FINAL.
SEAMAN
THE CLUB'S DIRECTORS MET TO CONSIDER WHO SHOULD BE INVITED TO BE THE NEXT MANAGER...
I THINK WE SHOULD ASK ARSENE WENGER...
ARSENE WHO?
HE'S A FRENCHMAN ...HAS A GOOD REPUTATION.
BUT NO EXPERIENCE OF ENGLISH FOOTBALL...
WE DON'T NEED A CONTINENTAL NOBODY...
I SAY WE OFFER BRUCE RIOCH THE JOB. HE'S SAFE...
IT WAS RIOCH WHO BROUGHT DUTCHMAN DENNIS BERGKAMP TO HIGHBURY, AND ENGLAND'S DAVID PLATT FROM SAMPDORIA.
BERGKAMP PROVED A WONDERFUL ACQUISITION, HIS BEAUTIFUL FOOTBALL QUICKLY ENDEARING HIM TO THE HIGHBURY FAITHFUL.
ARSENAL FINISHED FIFTH IN THE PREMIER LEAGUE, WHICH WAS STILL A DISAPPOINTMENT TO THEIR FANS, SO RIOCH'S REIGN WAS SHORT...
ARSENE WHO?
WENGER APPOINTED
BUT THIS TIME ARSENAL HAD GOT EXACTLY THE RIGHT MAN...
IN 1997 ARSENE WENGER ADDED ANOTHER DUTCH PLAYER, MARC OVERMARS, TO HIS SQUAD...

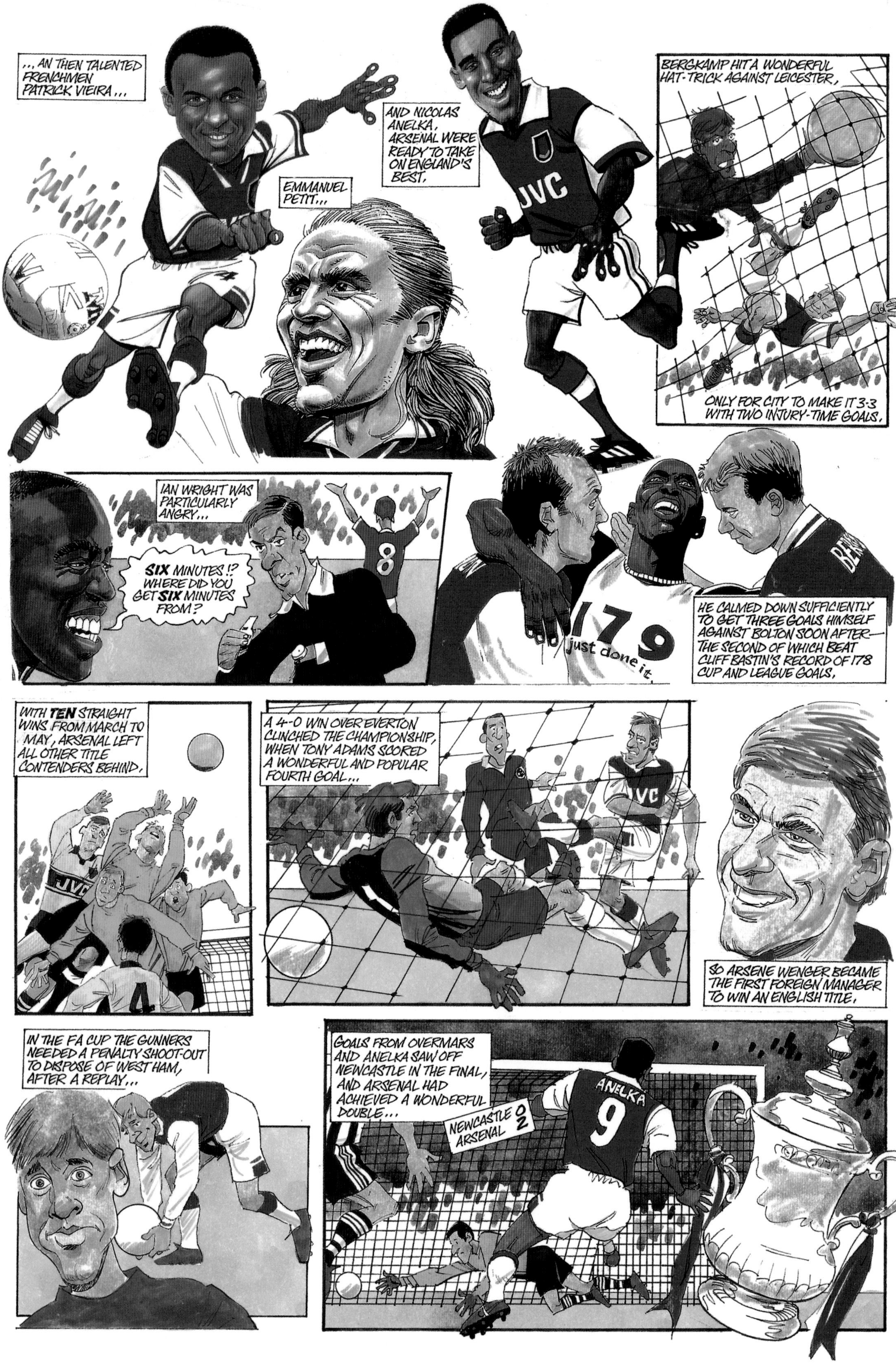

..., AN THEN TALENTED FRENCHMEN PATRICK VIEIRA...
EMMANUEL PETIT...
AND NICOLAS ANELKA, ARSENAL WERE READY TO TAKE ON ENGLAND'S BEST.
JVC
BERGKAMP HIT A WONDERFUL HAT-TRICK AGAINST LEICESTER,
ONLY FOR CITY TO MAKE IT 3-3 WITH TWO INJURY-TIME GOALS.
IAN WRIGHT WAS PARTICULARLY ANGRY...
SIX MINUTES !? WHERE DID YOU GET SIX MINUTES FROM?
8
179
just done it.
HE CALMED DOWN SUFFICIENTLY TO GET THREE GOALS HIMSELF AGAINST BOLTON SOON AFTER— THE SECOND OF WHICH BEAT CLIFF BASTIN'S RECORD OF 178 CUP AND LEAGUE GOALS.
WITH TEN STRAIGHT WINS FROM MARCH TO MAY, ARSENAL LEFT ALL OTHER TITLE CONTENDERS BEHIND.
JVC
A 4-0 WIN OVER EVERTON CLINCHED THE CHAMPIONSHIP, WHEN TONY ADAMS SCORED A WONDERFUL AND POPULAR FOURTH GOAL...
JVC
SO ARSENE WENGER BECAME THE FIRST FOREIGN MANAGER TO WIN AN ENGLISH TITLE.
IN THE FA CUP THE GUNNERS NEEDED A PENALTY SHOOT-OUT TO DISPOSE OF WEST HAM, AFTER A REPLAY...
GOALS FROM OVERMARS AND ANELKA SAW OFF NEWCASTLE IN THE FINAL, AND ARSENAL HAD ACHIEVED A WONDERFUL DOUBLE...
NEWCASTLE 0
ARSENAL 2
ANELKA
9

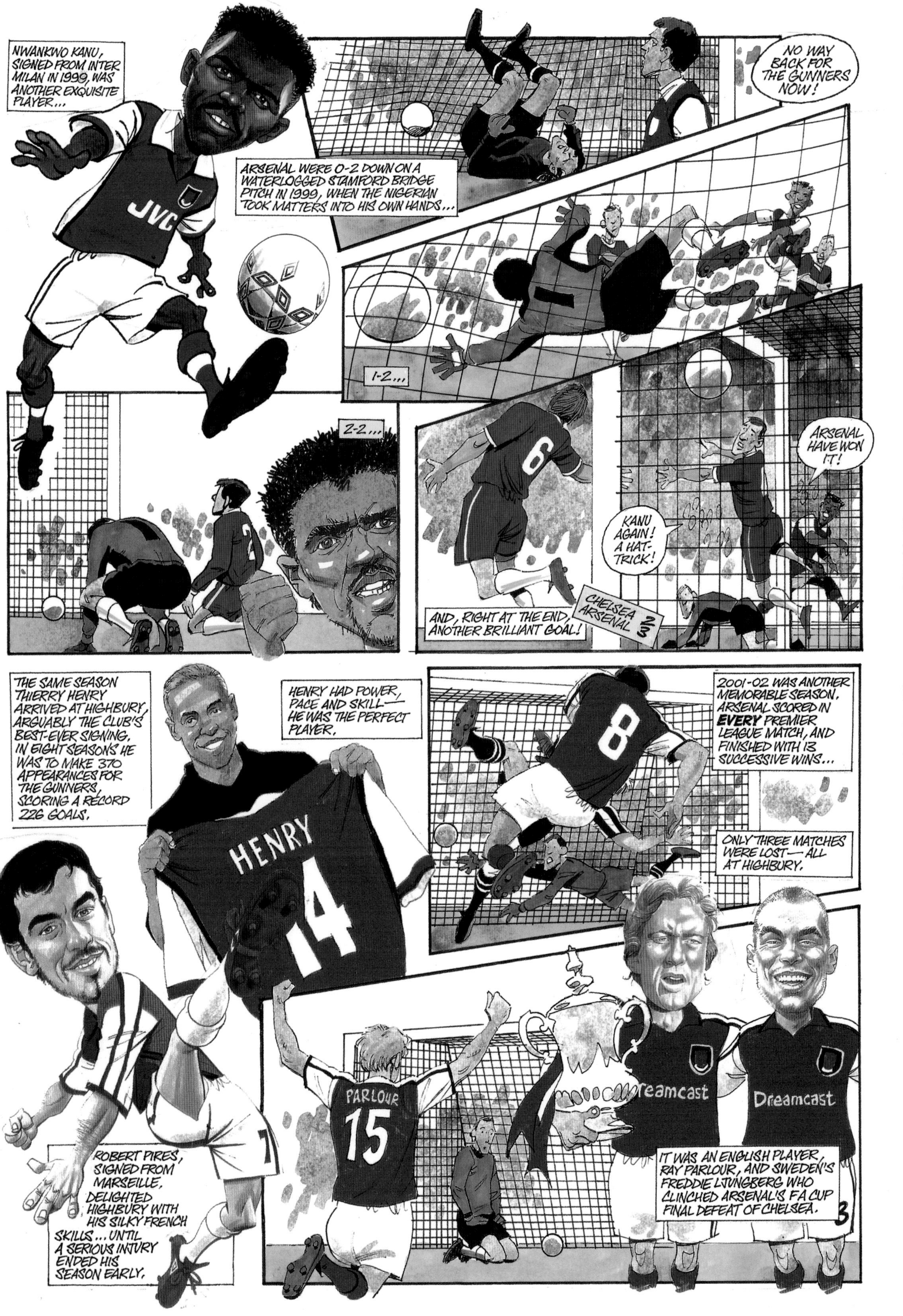
NWANKWO KANU, SIGNED FROM INTER MILAN IN 1999, WAS ANOTHER EXQUISITE PLAYER...
JVC
NO WAY BACK FOR THE GUNNERS NOW!
ARSENAL WERE 0-2 DOWN ON A WATERLOGGED STAMFORD BRIDGE PITCH IN 1999, WHEN THE NIGERIAN TOOK MATTERS INTO HIS OWN HANDS...
1-2...
2-2...
ARSENAL HAVE WON IT!
KANU AGAIN! A HAT-TRICK!
AND, RIGHT AT THE END, ANOTHER BRILLIANT GOAL!
CHELSEA 2
ARSENAL 3
THE SAME SEASON THIERRY HENRY ARRIVED AT HIGHBURY, ARGUABLY THE CLUB'S BEST-EVER SIGNING. IN EIGHT SEASONS HE WAS TO MAKE 370 APPEARANCES FOR THE GUNNERS, SCORING A RECORD 226 GOALS.
HENRY HAD POWER, PACE AND SKILL— HE WAS THE PERFECT PLAYER.
HENRY
14
2001-02 WAS ANOTHER MEMORABLE SEASON. ARSENAL SCORED IN EVERY PREMIER LEAGUE MATCH, AND FINISHED WITH 13 SUCCESSIVE WINS...
ONLY THREE MATCHES WERE LOST— ALL AT HIGHBURY.
PARLOUR
15
Dreamcast
Dreamcast
ROBERT PIRES, SIGNED FROM MARSEILLE, DELIGHTED HIGHBURY WITH HIS SILKY FRENCH SKILLS... UNTIL A SERIOUS INJURY ENDED HIS SEASON EARLY.
IT WAS AN ENGLISH PLAYER, RAY PARLOUR, AND SWEDEN'S FREDDIE LJUNGBERG WHO CLINCHED ARSENAL'S FA CUP FINAL DEFEAT OF CHELSEA.

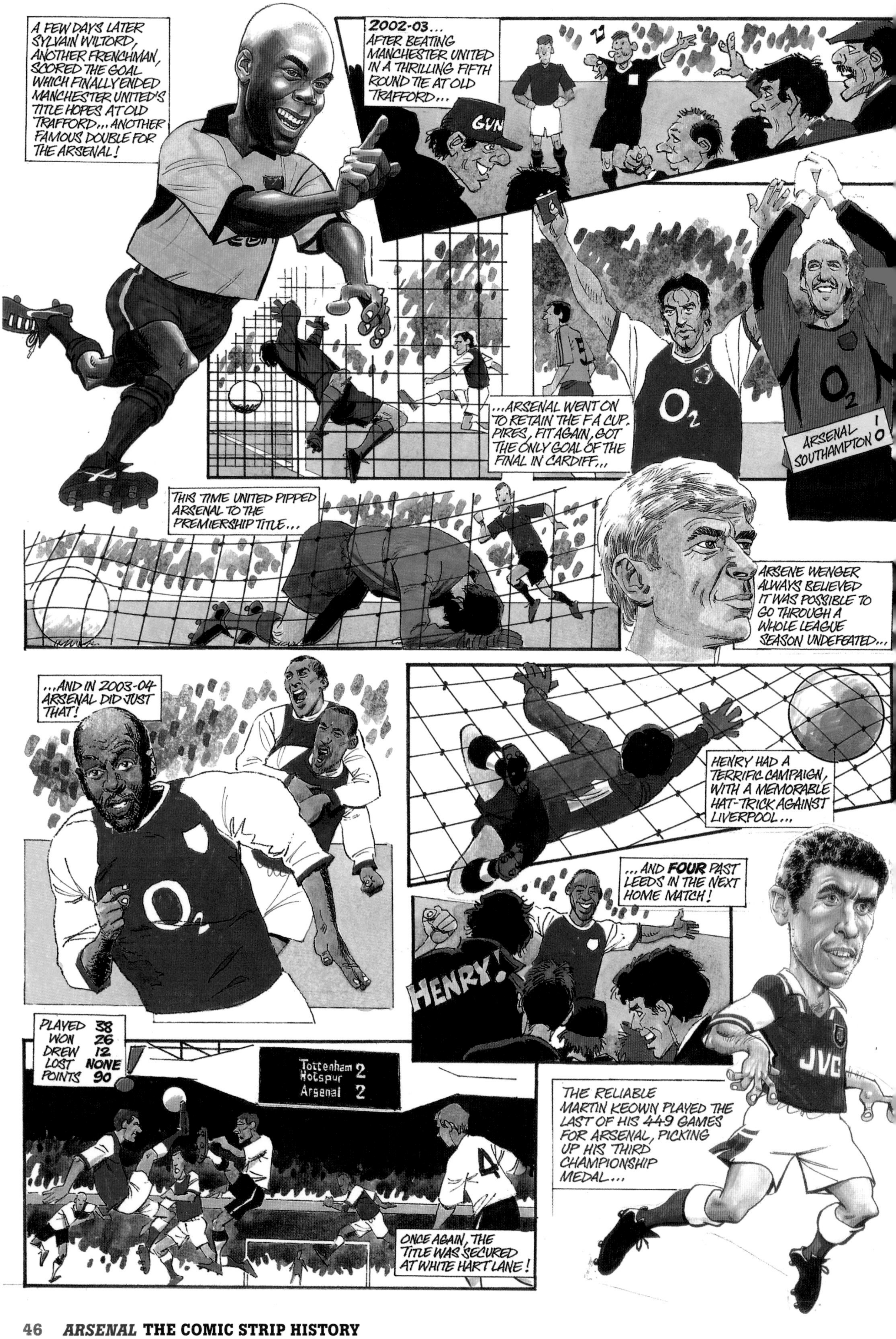

A FEW DAYS LATER SYLVAIN WILTORD, ANOTHER FRENCHMAN, SCORED THE GOAL WHICH FINALLY ENDED MANCHESTER UNITED'S TITLE HOPES AT OLD TRAFFORD... ANOTHER FAMOUS DOUBLE FOR THE ARSENAL!
2002-03... AFTER BEATING MANCHESTER UNITED IN A THRILLING FIFTH ROUND TIE AT OLD TRAFFORD...
GUN
...ARSENAL WENT ON TO RETAIN THE F A CUP. PIRES, FIT AGAIN, GOT THE ONLY GOAL OF THE FINAL IN CARDIFF...
ARSENAL 1
SOUTHAMPTON 0
THIS TIME UNITED PIPPED ARSENAL TO THE PREMIERSHIP TITLE...
ARSENE WENGER ALWAYS BELIEVED IT WAS POSSIBLE TO GO THROUGH A WHOLE LEAGUE SEASON UNDEFEATED...
...AND IN 2003-04 ARSENAL DID JUST THAT!
HENRY HAD A TERRIFIC CAMPAIGN, WITH A MEMORABLE HAT-TRICK AGAINST LIVERPOOL...
...AND FOUR PAST LEEDS IN THE NEXT HOME MATCH!
HENRY!
PLAYED 38
WON 26
DREW 12
LOST NONE
POINTS 90
!
Tottenham Hotspur 2
Arsenal 2
ONCE AGAIN, THE TITLE WAS SECURED AT WHITE HART LANE!
JVC
THE RELIABLE MARTIN KEOWN PLAYED THE LAST OF HIS 449 GAMES FOR ARSENAL, PICKING UP HIS THIRD CHAMPIONSHIP MEDAL...

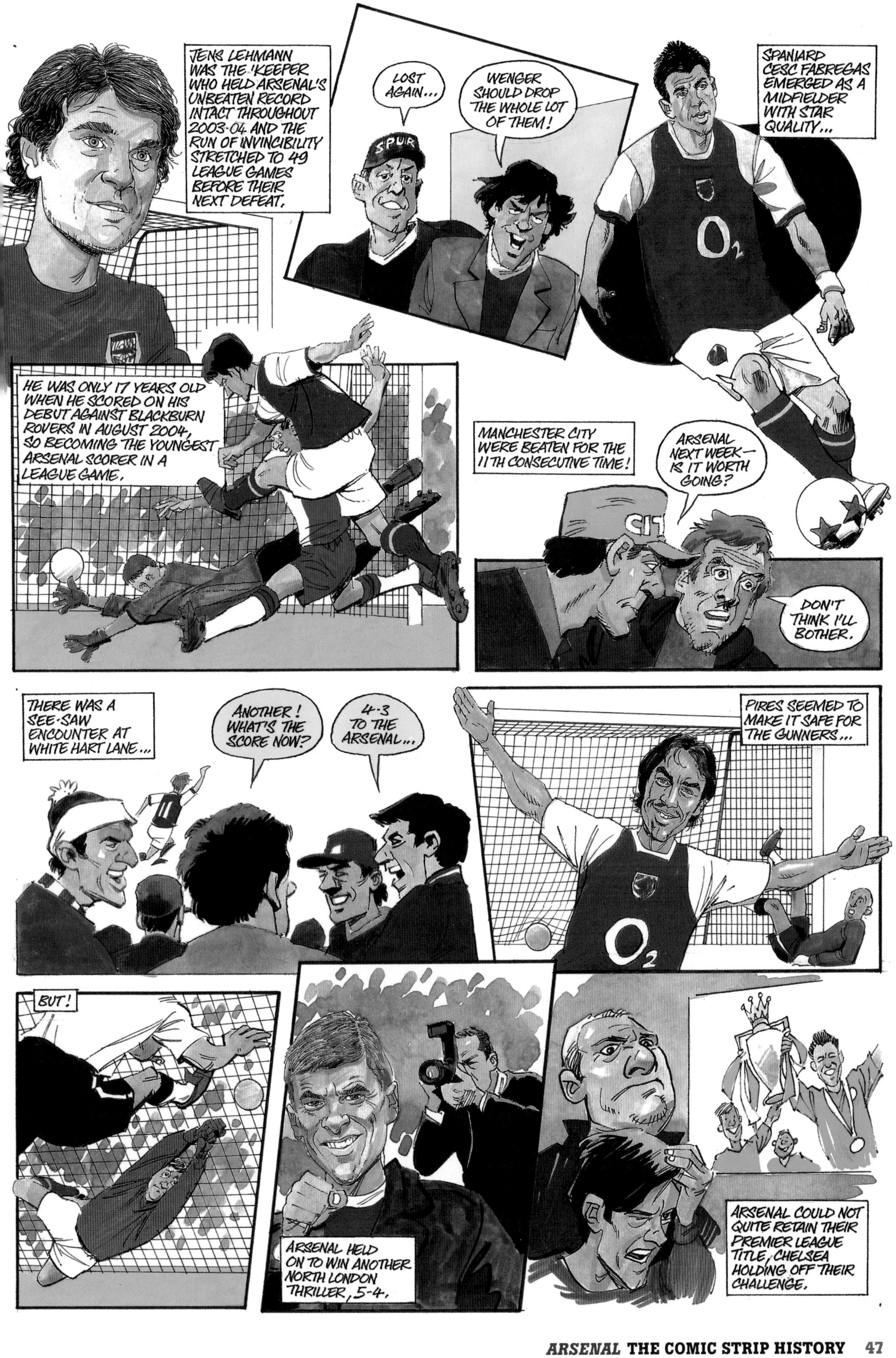
JENS LEHMANN WAS THE 'KEEPER WHO HELD ARSENAL'S UNBEATEN RECORD INTACT THROUGHOUT 2003-04 AND THE RUN OF INVINCIBILITY STRETCHED TO 49 LEAGUE GAMES BEFORE THEIR NEXT DEFEAT.
LOST AGAIN...
WENGER SHOULD DROP THE WHOLE LOT OF THEM!
SPUR
SPANIARD CESC FABREGAS EMERGED AS A MIDFIELDER WITH STAR QUALITY...
O2
HE WAS ONLY 17 YEARS OLD WHEN HE SCORED ON HIS DEBUT AGAINST BLACKBURN ROVERS IN AUGUST 2004, SO BECOMING THE YOUNGEST ARSENAL SCORER IN A LEAGUE GAME.
MANCHESTER CITY WERE BEATEN FOR THE 11TH CONSECUTIVE TIME!
ARSENAL NEXT WEEK— IS IT WORTH GOING?
DON'T THINK I'LL BOTHER.
THERE WAS A SEE-SAW ENCOUNTER AT WHITE HART LANE...
ANOTHER! WHAT'S THE SCORE NOW?
4-3 TO THE ARSENAL...
PIRES SEEMED TO MAKE IT SAFE FOR THE GUNNERS...
O2
BUT!
ARSENAL HELD ON TO WIN ANOTHER NORTH LONDON THRILLER, 5-4.
ARSENAL COULD NOT QUITE RETAIN THEIR PREMIER LEAGUE TITLE, CHELSEA HOLDING OFF THEIR CHALLENGE.

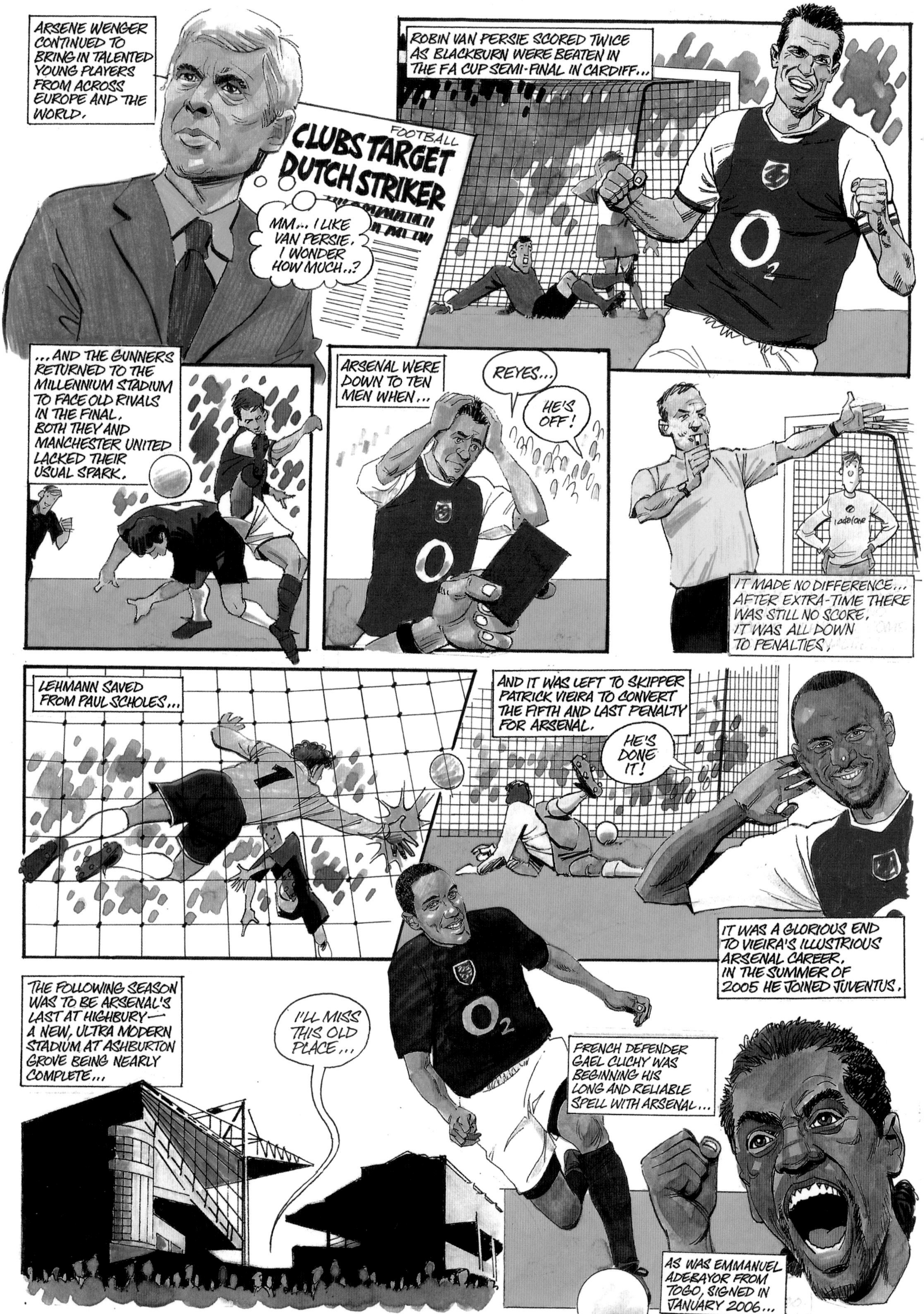

ARSENE WENGER CONTINUED TO BRING IN TALENTED YOUNG PLAYERS FROM ACROSS EUROPE AND THE WORLD.
FOOTBALL
CLUBS TARGET DUTCH STRIKER
MM... I LIKE VAN PERSIE. I WONDER HOW MUCH..?
ROBIN VAN PERSIE SCORED TWICE AS BLACKBURN WERE BEATEN IN THE FA CUP SEMI-FINAL IN CARDIFF...
...AND THE GUNNERS RETURNED TO THE MILLENNIUM STADIUM TO FACE OLD RIVALS IN THE FINAL. BOTH THEY AND MANCHESTER UNITED LACKED THEIR USUAL SPARK.
ARSENAL WERE DOWN TO TEN MEN WHEN...
REYES...
HE'S OFF!
IT MADE NO DIFFERENCE... AFTER EXTRA-TIME THERE WAS STILL NO SCORE. IT WAS ALL DOWN TO PENALTIES.
LEHMANN SAVED FROM PAUL SCHOLES...
AND IT WAS LEFT TO SKIPPER PATRICK VIEIRA TO CONVERT THE FIFTH AND LAST PENALTY FOR ARSENAL.
HE'S DONE IT!
IT WAS A GLORIOUS END TO VIEIRA'S ILLUSTRIOUS ARSENAL CAREER. IN THE SUMMER OF 2005 HE JOINED JUVENTUS.
THE FOLLOWING SEASON WAS TO BE ARSENAL'S LAST AT HIGHBURY— A NEW, ULTRA MODERN STADIUM AT ASHBURTON GROVE BEING NEARLY COMPLETE...
I'LL MISS THIS OLD PLACE...
FRENCH DEFENDER GAEL CLICHY WAS BEGINNING HIS LONG AND RELIABLE SPELL WITH ARSENAL...
AS WAS EMMANUEL ADEBAYOR FROM TOGO, SIGNED IN JANUARY 2006...

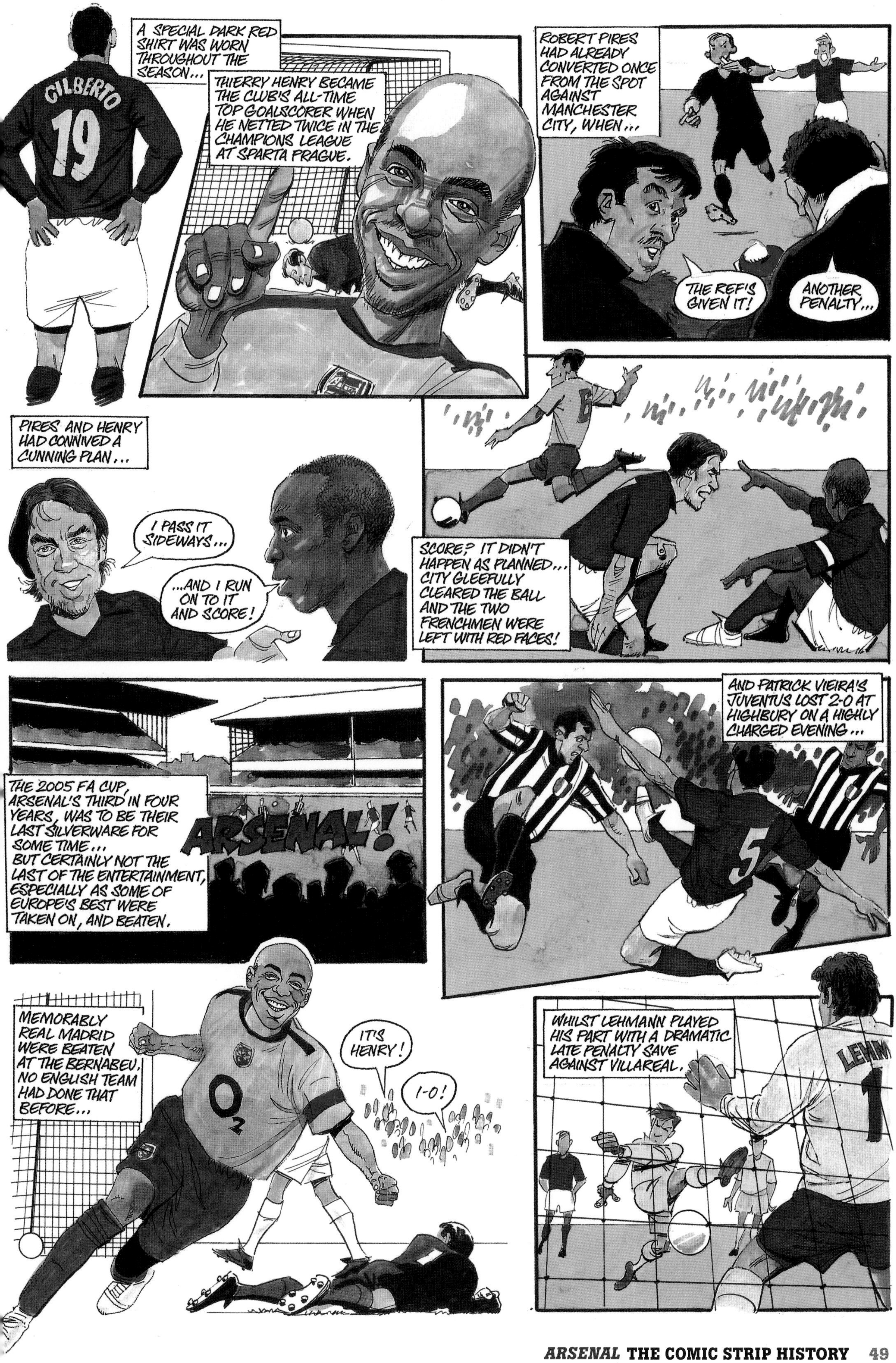

GILBERTO
19
A SPECIAL DARK RED SHIRT WAS WORN THROUGHOUT THE SEASON...
THIERRY HENRY BECAME THE CLUB'S ALL-TIME TOP GOALSCORER WHEN HE NETTED TWICE IN THE CHAMPIONS LEAGUE AT SPARTA PRAGUE.
ROBERT PIRES HAD ALREADY CONVERTED ONCE FROM THE SPOT AGAINST MANCHESTER CITY, WHEN...
THE REF'S GIVEN IT!
ANOTHER PENALTY...
PIRES AND HENRY HAD CONNIVED A CUNNING PLAN...
I PASS IT SIDEWAYS...
...AND I RUN ON TO IT AND SCORE!
SCORE? IT DIDN'T HAPPEN AS PLANNED... CITY GLEEFULLY CLEARED THE BALL AND THE TWO FRENCHMEN WERE LEFT WITH RED FACES!
THE 2005 FA CUP, ARSENAL'S THIRD IN FOUR YEARS, WAS TO BE THEIR LAST SILVERWARE FOR SOME TIME... BUT CERTAINLY NOT THE LAST OF THE ENTERTAINMENT, ESPECIALLY AS SOME OF EUROPE'S BEST WERE TAKEN ON, AND BEATEN.
ARSENAL!
AND PATRICK VIEIRA'S JUVENTUS LOST 2-0 AT HIGHBURY ON A HIGHLY CHARGED EVENING...
5
MEMORABLY REAL MADRID WERE BEATEN AT THE BERNABEU, NO ENGLISH TEAM HAD DONE THAT BEFORE...
IT'S HENRY!
1-0!
O2
WHILST LEHMANN PLAYED HIS PART WITH A DRAMATIC LATE PENALTY SAVE AGAINST VILLAREAL.
LEHM
1

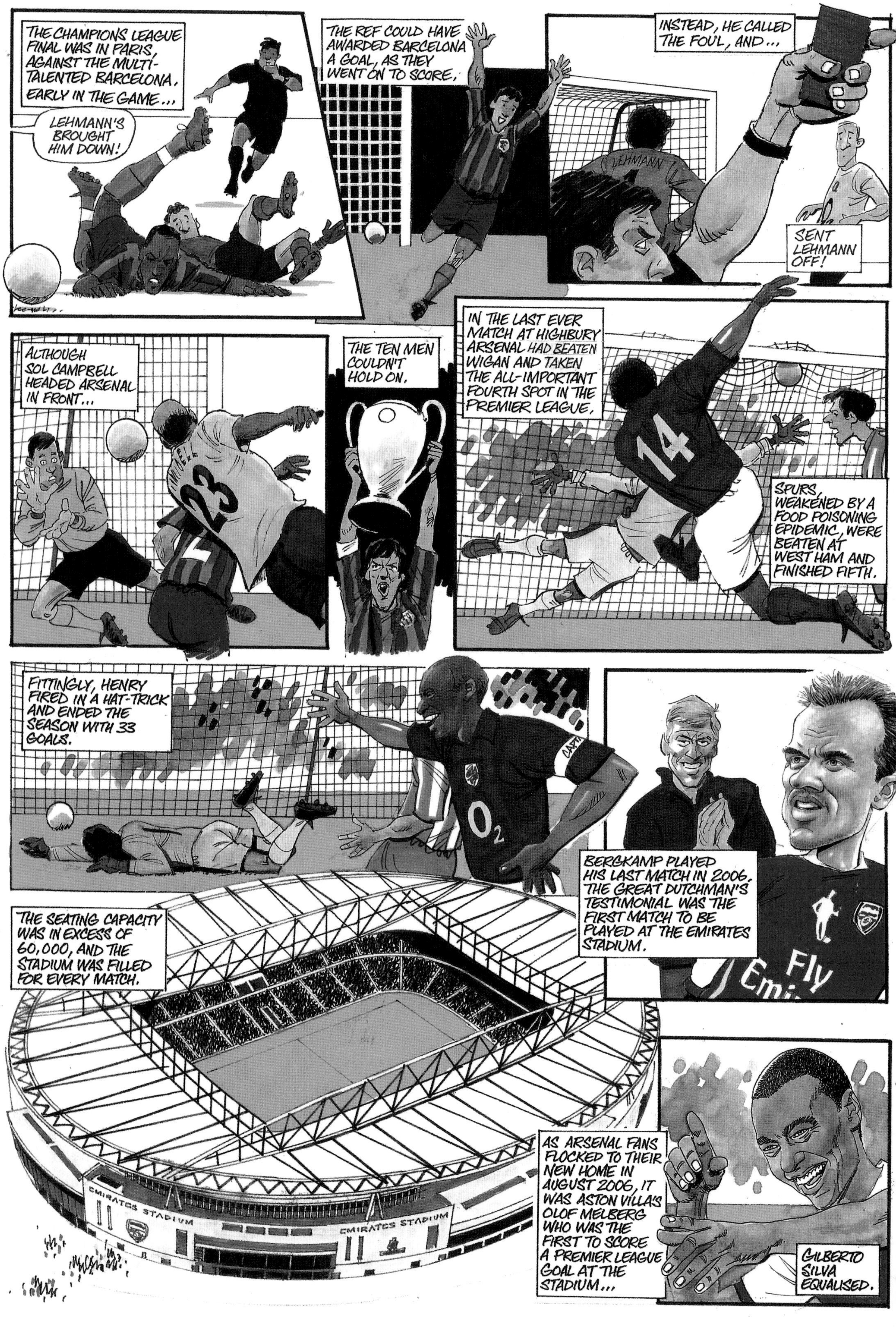
THE CHAMPIONS LEAGUE FINAL WAS IN PARIS, AGAINST THE MULTI-TALENTED BARCELONA. EARLY IN THE GAME...
LEHMANN'S BROUGHT HIM DOWN!
THE REF COULD HAVE AWARDED BARCELONA A GOAL, AS THEY WENT ON TO SCORE.
INSTEAD, HE CALLED THE FOUL, AND...
LEHMANN
SENT LEHMANN OFF!
ALTHOUGH SOL CAMPBELL HEADED ARSENAL IN FRONT...
THE TEN MEN COULDN'T HOLD ON.
IN THE LAST EVER MATCH AT HIGHBURY ARSENAL HAD BEATEN WIGAN AND TAKEN THE ALL-IMPORTANT FOURTH SPOT IN THE PREMIER LEAGUE.
SPURS, WEAKENED BY A FOOD POISONING EPIDEMIC, WERE BEATEN AT WEST HAM AND FINISHED FIFTH.
FITTINGLY, HENRY FIRED IN A HAT-TRICK AND ENDED THE SEASON WITH 33 GOALS.
BERGKAMP PLAYED HIS LAST MATCH IN 2006. THE GREAT DUTCHMAN'S TESTIMONIAL WAS THE FIRST MATCH TO BE PLAYED AT THE EMIRATES STADIUM.
Fly Emi
THE SEATING CAPACITY WAS IN EXCESS OF 60,000, AND THE STADIUM WAS FILLED FOR EVERY MATCH.
EMIRATES STADIUM
EMIRATES STADIUM
AS ARSENAL FANS FLOCKED TO THEIR NEW HOME IN AUGUST 2006, IT WAS ASTON VILLA'S OLOF MELBERG WHO WAS THE FIRST TO SCORE A PREMIER LEAGUE GOAL AT THE STADIUM...
GILBERTO SILVA EQUALISED.

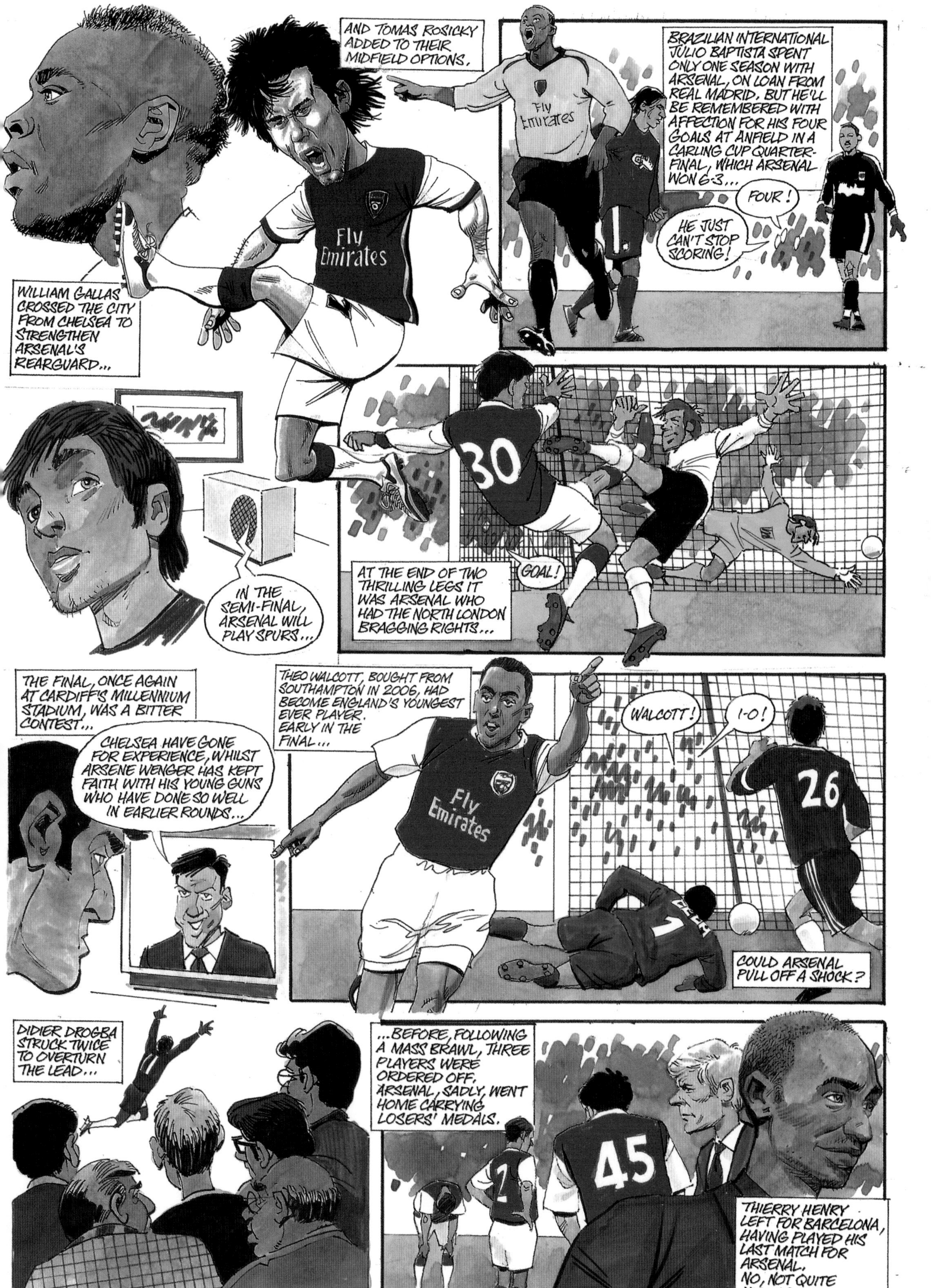
WILLIAM GALLAS CROSSED THE CITY FROM CHELSEA TO STRENGTHEN ARSENAL'S REARGUARD...
AND TOMAS ROSICKY ADDED TO THEIR MIDFIELD OPTIONS.
Fly Emirates
BRAZILIAN INTERNATIONAL JULIO BAPTISTA SPENT ONLY ONE SEASON WITH ARSENAL, ON LOAN FROM REAL MADRID, BUT HE'LL BE REMEMBERED WITH AFFECTION FOR HIS FOUR GOALS AT ANFIELD IN A CARLING CUP QUARTER-FINAL, WHICH ARSENAL WON 6-3...
FOUR!
HE JUST CAN'T STOP SCORING!
IN THE SEMI-FINAL, ARSENAL WILL PLAY SPURS...
AT THE END OF TWO THRILLING LEGS IT WAS ARSENAL WHO HAD THE NORTH LONDON BRAGGING RIGHTS...
GOAL!
THE FINAL, ONCE AGAIN AT CARDIFF'S MILLENNIUM STADIUM, WAS A BITTER CONTEST...
CHELSEA HAVE GONE FOR EXPERIENCE, WHILST ARSENE WENGER HAS KEPT FAITH WITH HIS YOUNG GUNS WHO HAVE DONE SO WELL IN EARLIER ROUNDS...
THEO WALCOTT, BOUGHT FROM SOUTHAMPTON IN 2006, HAD BECOME ENGLAND'S YOUNGEST EVER PLAYER. EARLY IN THE FINAL...
WALCOTT!
1-0!
Fly Emirates
COULD ARSENAL PULL OFF A SHOCK?
DIDIER DROGBA STRUCK TWICE TO OVERTURN THE LEAD...
...BEFORE, FOLLOWING A MASS BRAWL, THREE PLAYERS WERE ORDERED OFF. ARSENAL, SADLY, WENT HOME CARRYING LOSERS' MEDALS.
THIERRY HENRY LEFT FOR BARCELONA, HAVING PLAYED HIS LAST MATCH FOR ARSENAL. NO, NOT QUITE HIS LAST...

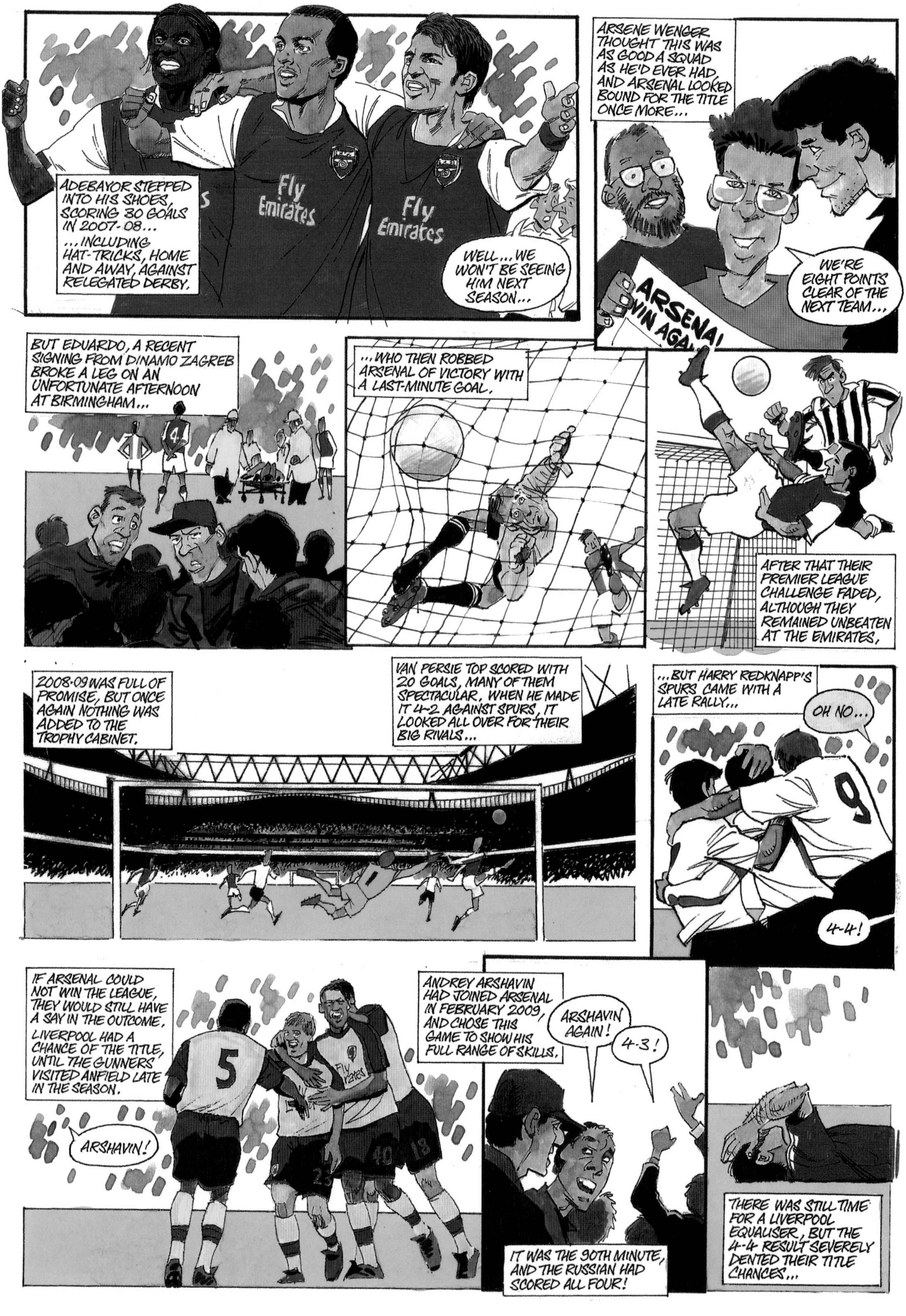

ADEBAYOR STEPPED INTO HIS SHOES, SCORING 30 GOALS IN 2007-08...
...INCLUDING HAT-TRICKS, HOME AND AWAY, AGAINST RELEGATED DERBY.
WELL... WE WON'T BE SEEING HIM NEXT SEASON...
Fly Emirates
Fly Emirates
ARSENE WENGER THOUGHT THIS WAS AS GOOD A SQUAD AS HE'D EVER HAD, AND ARSENAL LOOKED BOUND FOR THE TITLE ONCE MORE...
WE'RE EIGHT POINTS CLEAR OF THE NEXT TEAM...
ARSENAL WIN AGAIN
BUT EDUARDO, A RECENT SIGNING FROM DINAMO ZAGREB BROKE A LEG ON AN UNFORTUNATE AFTERNOON AT BIRMINGHAM...
...WHO THEN ROBBED ARSENAL OF VICTORY WITH A LAST-MINUTE GOAL.
AFTER THAT THEIR PREMIER LEAGUE CHALLENGE FADED, ALTHOUGH THEY REMAINED UNBEATEN AT THE EMIRATES.
2008-09 WAS FULL OF PROMISE, BUT ONCE AGAIN NOTHING WAS ADDED TO THE TROPHY CABINET.
VAN PERSIE TOP SCORED WITH 20 GOALS, MANY OF THEM SPECTACULAR. WHEN HE MADE IT 4-2 AGAINST SPURS, IT LOOKED ALL OVER FOR THEIR BIG RIVALS...
...BUT HARRY REDKNAPP'S SPURS CAME WITH A LATE RALLY...
OH NO...
4-4!
IF ARSENAL COULD NOT WIN THE LEAGUE, THEY WOULD STILL HAVE A SAY IN THE OUTCOME.
LIVERPOOL HAD A CHANCE OF THE TITLE, UNTIL THE GUNNERS VISITED ANFIELD LATE IN THE SEASON.
ARSHAVIN!
ANDREY ARSHAVIN HAD JOINED ARSENAL IN FEBRUARY 2009, AND CHOSE THIS GAME TO SHOW HIS FULL RANGE OF SKILLS.
ARSHAVIN AGAIN!
4-3!
IT WAS THE 90TH MINUTE, AND THE RUSSIAN HAD SCORED ALL FOUR!
THERE WAS STILL TIME FOR A LIVERPOOL EQUALISER, BUT THE 4-4 RESULT SEVERELY DENTED THEIR TITLE CHANCES...

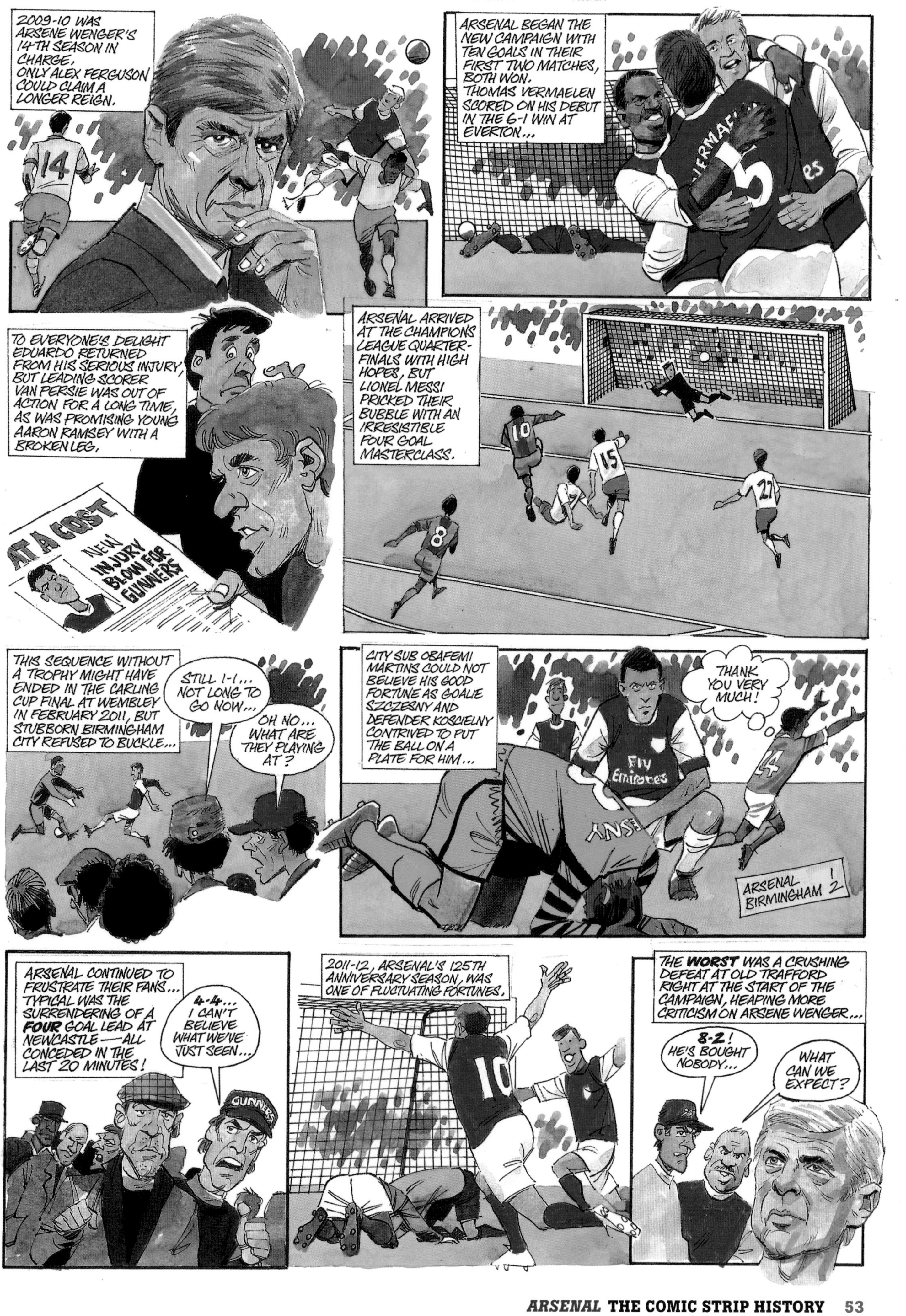
2009-10 WAS ARSENE WENGER'S 14TH SEASON IN CHARGE. ONLY ALEX FERGUSON COULD CLAIM A LONGER REIGN.
14
ARSENAL BEGAN THE NEW CAMPAIGN WITH TEN GOALS IN THEIR FIRST TWO MATCHES, BOTH WON. THOMAS VERMAELEN SCORED ON HIS DEBUT IN THE 6-1 WIN AT EVERTON...
TO EVERYONE'S DELIGHT EDUARDO RETURNED FROM HIS SERIOUS INJURY, BUT LEADING SCORER VAN PERSIE WAS OUT OF ACTION FOR A LONG TIME, AS WAS PROMISING YOUNG AARON RAMSEY WITH A BROKEN LEG.
AT A COST
NEW INJURY BLOW FOR GUNNERS
ARSENAL ARRIVED AT THE CHAMPIONS LEAGUE QUARTER-FINALS WITH HIGH HOPES, BUT LIONEL MESSI PRICKED THEIR BUBBLE WITH AN IRRESISTIBLE FOUR GOAL MASTERCLASS.
10
15
27
8
THIS SEQUENCE WITHOUT A TROPHY MIGHT HAVE ENDED IN THE CARLING CUP FINAL AT WEMBLEY IN FEBRUARY 2011, BUT STUBBORN BIRMINGHAM CITY REFUSED TO BUCKLE...
STILL 1-1... NOT LONG TO GO NOW...
OH NO... WHAT ARE THEY PLAYING AT?
CITY SUB OBAFEMI MARTINS COULD NOT BELIEVE HIS GOOD FORTUNE AS GOALIE SZCZESNY AND DEFENDER KOSCIELNY CONTRIVED TO PUT THE BALL ON A PLATE FOR HIM...
THANK YOU VERY MUCH!
Fly Emirates
ARSENAL 1
BIRMINGHAM 2
ARSENAL CONTINUED TO FRUSTRATE THEIR FANS... TYPICAL WAS THE SURRENDERING OF A FOUR GOAL LEAD AT NEWCASTLE—ALL CONCEDED IN THE LAST 20 MINUTES!
4-4... I CAN'T BELIEVE WHAT WE'VE JUST SEEN...
GUNNERS
2011-12, ARSENAL'S 125TH ANNIVERSARY SEASON, WAS ONE OF FLUCTUATING FORTUNES.
10
THE WORST WAS A CRUSHING DEFEAT AT OLD TRAFFORD RIGHT AT THE START OF THE CAMPAIGN, HEAPING MORE CRITICISM ON ARSENE WENGER...
8-2! HE'S BOUGHT NOBODY...
WHAT CAN WE EXPECT?

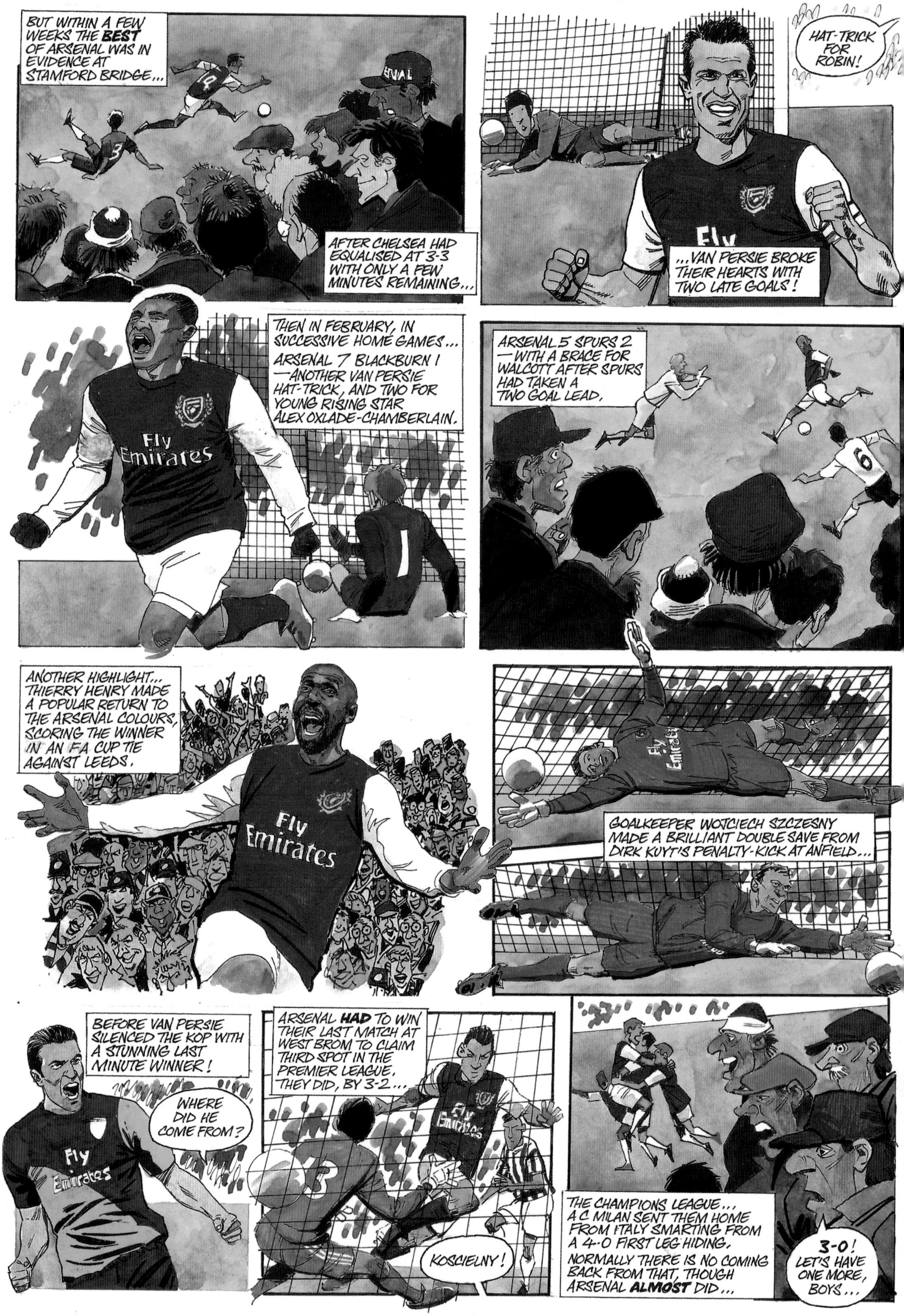
BUT WITHIN A FEW WEEKS THE **BEST** OF ARSENAL WAS IN EVIDENCE AT STAMFORD BRIDGE...
AFTER CHELSEA HAD EQUALISED AT 3-3 WITH ONLY A FEW MINUTES REMAINING...
HAT-TRICK FOR ROBIN!
...VAN PERSIE BROKE THEIR HEARTS WITH TWO LATE GOALS!
THEN IN FEBRUARY, IN SUCCESSIVE HOME GAMES...
ARSENAL 7 BLACKBURN 1 —ANOTHER VAN PERSIE HAT-TRICK, AND TWO FOR YOUNG RISING STAR ALEX OXLADE-CHAMBERLAIN.
ARSENAL 5 SPURS 2 — WITH A BRACE FOR WALCOTT AFTER SPURS HAD TAKEN A TWO GOAL LEAD.
ANOTHER HIGHLIGHT... THIERRY HENRY MADE A POPULAR RETURN TO THE ARSENAL COLOURS, SCORING THE WINNER IN AN FA CUP TIE AGAINST LEEDS.
GOALKEEPER WOJCIECH SZCZESNY MADE A BRILLIANT DOUBLE SAVE FROM DIRK KUYT'S PENALTY-KICK AT ANFIELD...
BEFORE VAN PERSIE SILENCED THE KOP WITH A STUNNING LAST MINUTE WINNER!
WHERE DID HE COME FROM?
ARSENAL **HAD** TO WIN THEIR LAST MATCH AT WEST BROM TO CLAIM THIRD SPOT IN THE PREMIER LEAGUE. THEY DID, BY 3-2...
KOSCIELNY!
THE CHAMPIONS LEAGUE... A C MILAN SENT THEM HOME FROM ITALY SMARTING FROM A 4-0 FIRST LEG HIDING.
NORMALLY THERE IS NO COMING BACK FROM THAT, THOUGH ARSENAL **ALMOST** DID...
3-0! LET'S HAVE ONE MORE, BOYS...

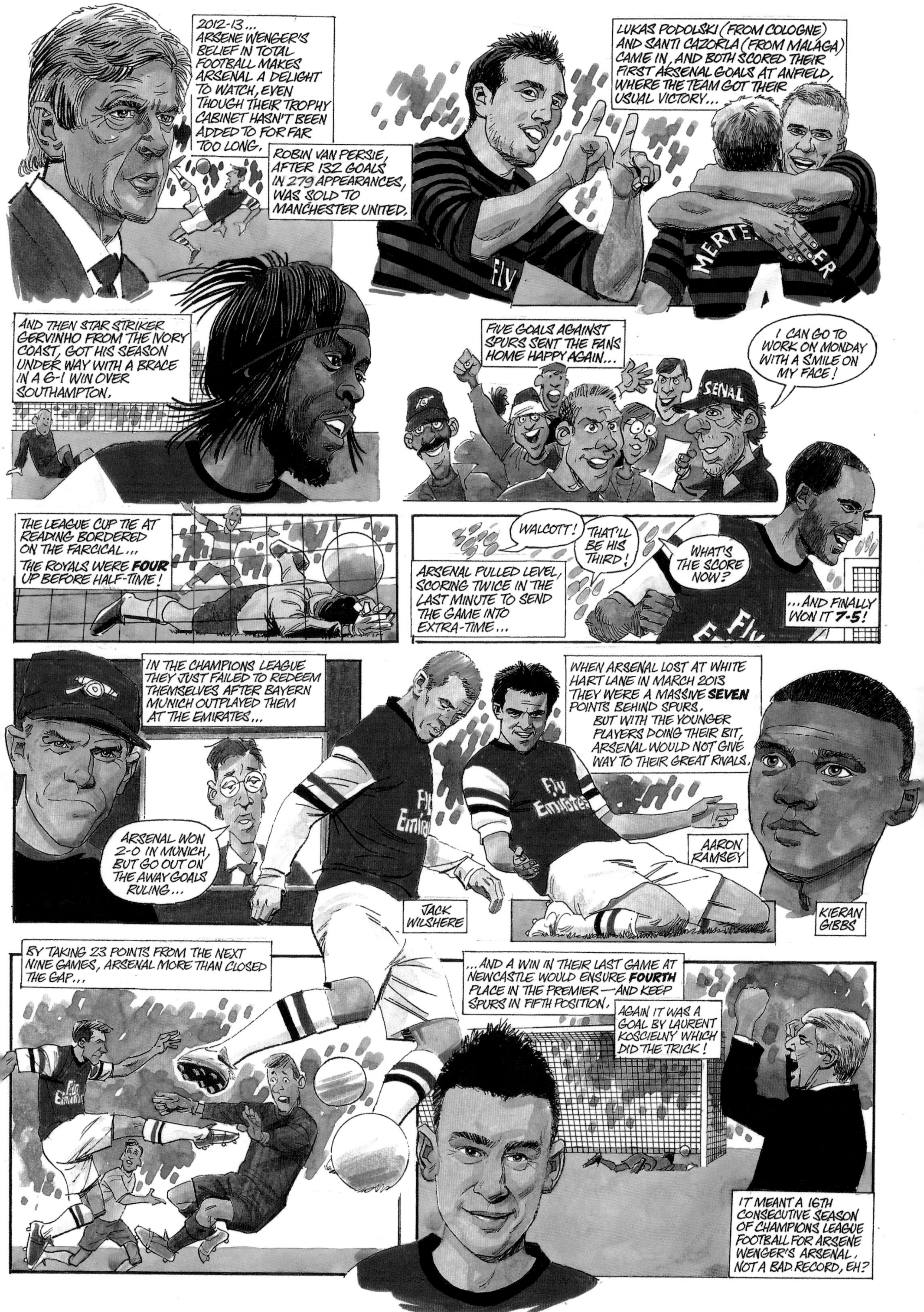
2012-13... ARSENE WENGER'S BELIEF IN TOTAL FOOTBALL MAKES ARSENAL A DELIGHT TO WATCH, EVEN THOUGH THEIR TROPHY CABINET HASN'T BEEN ADDED TO FOR FAR TOO LONG.
ROBIN VAN PERSIE, AFTER 132 GOALS IN 279 APPEARANCES, WAS SOLD TO MANCHESTER UNITED.
LUKAS PODOLSKI (FROM COLOGNE) AND SANTI CAZORLA (FROM MALAGA) CAME IN, AND BOTH SCORED THEIR FIRST ARSENAL GOALS AT ANFIELD, WHERE THE TEAM GOT THEIR USUAL VICTORY...
FLY
MERTE ER
AND THEN STAR STRIKER GERVINHO FROM THE IVORY COAST, GOT HIS SEASON UNDER WAY WITH A BRACE IN A 6-1 WIN OVER SOUTHAMPTON.
FIVE GOALS AGAINST SPURS SENT THE FANS HOME HAPPY AGAIN...
I CAN GO TO WORK ON MONDAY WITH A SMILE ON MY FACE!
SENAL
THE LEAGUE CUP TIE AT READING BORDERED ON THE FARCICAL... THE ROYALS WERE FOUR UP BEFORE HALF-TIME!
WALCOTT!
THAT'LL BE HIS THIRD!
WHAT'S THE SCORE NOW?
ARSENAL PULLED LEVEL, SCORING TWICE IN THE LAST MINUTE TO SEND THE GAME INTO EXTRA-TIME...
...AND FINALLY WON IT 7-5!
IN THE CHAMPIONS LEAGUE THEY JUST FAILED TO REDEEM THEMSELVES AFTER BAYERN MUNICH OUTPLAYED THEM AT THE EMIRATES...
ARSENAL WON 2-0 IN MUNICH, BUT GO OUT ON THE AWAY GOALS RULING...
WHEN ARSENAL LOST AT WHITE HART LANE IN MARCH 2013 THEY WERE A MASSIVE SEVEN POINTS BEHIND SPURS.
BUT WITH THE YOUNGER PLAYERS DOING THEIR BIT, ARSENAL WOULD NOT GIVE WAY TO THEIR GREAT RIVALS.
Fly Emirates
AARON RAMSEY
JACK WILSHERE
KIERAN GIBBS
BY TAKING 23 POINTS FROM THE NEXT NINE GAMES, ARSENAL MORE THAN CLOSED THE GAP...
...AND A WIN IN THEIR LAST GAME AT NEWCASTLE WOULD ENSURE FOURTH PLACE IN THE PREMIER — AND KEEP SPURS IN FIFTH POSITION.
AGAIN IT WAS A GOAL BY LAURENT KOSCIELNY WHICH DID THE TRICK!
IT MEANT A 16TH CONSECUTIVE SEASON OF CHAMPIONS LEAGUE FOOTBALL FOR ARSENE WENGER'S ARSENAL. NOT A BAD RECORD, EH?